Annelie's
RAW FOOD POWER

supercharged raw food recipes and remedies

Annelie's RAW FOOD POWER

supercharged raw food recipes and remedies

Annelie Whitfield

Published by
Adams Media, a division of F+W Media, Inc.
57 Littlefield Street, Avon, MA 02322. U.S.A.
www.adamsmedia.com

ISBN-10: 1-4405-5751-9
ISBN-13: 978-1-4405-5751-4
eISBN-10: 1-4405-5752-7
eISBN-13: 978-1-4405-5752-1

Printed in China

Color origination by Ivy Press Reprographics

10 9 8 7 6 5 4 3 2 1

Library of Congress Cataloging-in-Publication Data
is available from the publisher.

This book was conceived, designed, and produced by
Ivy Press

Creative Director Peter Bridgewater
Publisher Susan Kelly
Art Director Wayne Blades
Senior Editor Jayne Ansell
Design, Art Direction & Styling Simon Daley
Jungle Photographer Jennifer Harter
Food Photographer Ian Garlick
Home Economist Lorna Brash

All spoon and cup measurements are level: 1 teaspoon is
assumed to be 5 ml, 1 tablespoon is assumed to
be 15 ml, and 1 cup is assumed to be 250 ml.

Always follow safety and commonsense cooking protocol while
using kitchen utensils, operating ovens and stoves, and handling
uncooked food. If children are assisting in the preparation of any
recipe, they should always be supervised by an adult.

CONTENTS

6 Preface—my journey

10 Making the transition to raw food

11 Recommended equipment

12 breakfast

38 lunch

60 snacks & treats

88 dinner

112 remedies

126 Suppliers, recommended reading, and useful websites

127 Index

128 Acknowledgments

PREFACE

my journey

Of all the gifts I received in my life, the most important was my childhood. I was always out and about, eating wild foods and loving the freedom of growing up on a farm. My early years were spent mostly barefoot and, today, I'm delighted to be able to gift my children the grounded, barefoot magic of living close to nature.

When I was four I decided that I was going to become a stunt girl, and from the age of twenty-three I found myself doubling for the likes of Julia Roberts, Nicole Kidman, and Cameron Diaz. I spent seven years jumping off bridges, being beaten up and set on fire, and crashing cars. It was a wonderful but brief career, full of excitement, travel, fun, and a fair amount of fear. However, deep down I always knew that one day I would be spending more time in nature, and I'd be doing something more likely to nurture my health than threaten it!

My turning time point came four years down the line, when I had a serious car crash while working, which left me burned, battered, and somewhat disillusioned. This, of course, was a blessing in disguise and the shake up I needed to start me on a different journey. I spent almost a year healing, choosing natural alternatives to conventional medicine where possible, because it felt so instinctively wrong to be mummified in casts and be applying strong pharmaceutical creams. This year was a time of huge learning, which left me both humbled and in awe of the power of herbs, living foods, plant spirits, bone-mending monks, homeopathy, Chinese medicine, and much, much more.

the here and now

I am now a qualified naturopath and herbalist and have spent the last eight years running clinics, presenting TV shows, and traveling the world in search of powerful natural remedies and recipes.

I am not exactly sure why, but I have always had a deep-seated pull toward the jungle, which has intensified as I've traveled. I have spent many years reading about jungle medicine and am fascinated by people's journeys into the jungles of the world; books, such as *Jungle Medicine* by Connie Grauds and *The Healing Power of Rainforest Herbs* by Leslie Taylor, ND, inspire me.

Then, one day, came the realization that my inspirations were just voyeurism—I wasn't living those experiences. How had it come to pass that the "nature girl" I so cherished inside had become part of the furniture in London's urban jungle? In a remarkably casual conversation, given the gravitas of what we were discussing, my husband Jamie and I decided that same night to completely change our lives. We wanted to remove our little girls from the big city into a more natural living environment, learn a new language, experience a completely different culture, and no longer be in a nine-to-five existence. After a few months of plotting and planning, selling our house, and putting more than ten years of London life into storage, we went to live in the Costa Rican jungle. It was many things, from sheer bliss to borderline hell, but it was always highly stimulating.

The journey taught me so much, not just about how incredible it is to experience living such a different life, but also about my family. I feel like I know each one of them so much better, and I now understand how such an experience can strengthen ideas about how you want to live your life. It also taught me something that I always knew, but hadn't yet properly experienced: the power of the natural world. Living so close to nature was at times intimidating and a real challenge, but also incredibly energizing.

As a health practitioner, I have spent many years learning from courses, books, and seminars. But from living in the jungle I have changed some of my previous ideas about diet and lifestyle, and I now feel that I know how I really want to live, what I want to eat, and most importantly, how to nurture my children. I have no doubt in my mind that taking my kids out of the urban jungle and into the real one has been truly amazing for their little spirits, nourishing and supporting them while they rise to the challenges of life.

I wrote this book to share my experiences of the transition we have made, the recipes and remedies I have used along the way, and the herbal, nutritional, and lifestyle knowledge that I have learned during this time. I am deeply passionate about feeling alive and creative, and hope I can inspire you to feel this way by making the best choices for your mind and body, wherever you live.

"Be weird. Be random. Be who you are. Because you would never know who would love the person you hide." Unknown

my raw food journey

I have always gravitated toward healthy food, and eating fresh, wild, seasonal food has been a deep-seated passion for many years. Before I became a fan of raw foods, I had spent many years experimenting with vegetarianism and veganism, supplementing with an array of nutrient-rich foods and herbs and experiencing the importance of 100 percent organic. However, the transition to raw happened when I experienced that inevitable exhaustion from having my first baby. The endless nights breastfeeding and dealing with a challenging child drained all my resources, so after talking to a raw foodie friend who claimed to need only four hours sleep a night due to his high raw diet I thought, "That's it, I'm going *all* raw."

This was, without a doubt, one of the best choices I ever made. I felt better, looked better; I felt more energized. I spent less time feeling like a crazily hungry, breastfeeding mom because all the raw food snacks were so nutritionally packed. I also spent less time thinking about what to eat and prepare. I lived off superfood shakes, green and seaweed salads, dehydrated crackers, dips, and loads of raw chocolate; it just felt easy! And my little baby girl *loved* it! More breast milk, more calmness of spirit, and of course a happier mama!

I continued along this path in my next pregnancy and kept both my little girls "in the raw" until the age of two, when they naturally became curious about other foods. I've allowed them to make their own choices about whether to eat a wholly raw food diet, and luckily they have very healthy palates; they are happy to eat raw and steamed vegetables, fruit, nut milks, raw dips, an abundance of green juices, raw crackers, smoothies, and other superfoods.

My journey into raw food has certainly been the catalyst for a broader understanding of nature and a desire to experience as much as possible in its unadulterated form.

making the transition to raw food

My advice to anyone interested in converting to a diet rich in raw food is not to put pressure on yourself. Like anything in life, it is a personal journey and will evolve while you find your right dietary balance. It is also a way of eating that must inspire, so if you are eager to introduce your family and friends to raw food, start them slowly with some of the delicious inventions in this book! Raw chocolate, dips, and crackers are a great way to introduce people to raw food. It is a different way of eating compared to the standard diet, however, and people can see it as restrictive. This, of course, is entirely untrue if you love eating highly nutritious, living foods, because, wherever you are, something is always available.

My diet changes as I experience different cultures, travel, and, of course, become older. My eating patterns have changed from only six months ago. Currently, I am juicing a lot of wild greens, making a lot of superfood smoothies, enjoying eggs and raw cheeses, and also eating some cooked foods, such as brown rice, quinoa, and steamed vegetables. Consuming just 50 percent raw with additional wild and nutrient-rich foods gives you a great upgrade in health, so this might be your starting point or maybe your perfect balance. My husband found his way into raw food through drinking green smoothies and was inspired by raw food expert and author Victoria Boutenko. He does a lot of traveling, and, although he doesn't maintain a 100 percent raw food diet, he keeps himself healthy and grounded via the huge amount of varied greens he consumes. This is his perfect balance.

I am passionate about our power as individuals and how we must never let food, healthy or unhealthy, get in the way of our full potential. I believe that when you are truly on the right life path, you will be attracted to all the right things for *you*.

recommended equipment

If you are looking to introduce raw food into your diet, I would thoroughly recommend investing in the following equipment. They have become essential items in my own kitchen, and I even take some of them traveling. Although the initial outlay might be expensive, you'll reap the benefits nutritionally and will have a lot of fun creating new and exciting raw food recipes.

Blender Vitamix and NutriBullet blenders are the best brands to buy. The Vitamix is perfect for the house, and the NutriBullet is your best friend if traveling.

Excalibur dehydrator This is well worth the expense if you have decided to switch to a raw food diet. It is a fabulous, lightweight second oven, which is great for making your weekly supply of crackers, breads, and cereals.

Juicer I love the Champion brand, but other commercial brands, such as Braun or Waring, are also good. Vegetable juices are an essential part of raw food nutrition and bring a deeper level of hydration to the body, so a juicer is a real must!

Food processor This is great for making raw pâtés and raw pastry dough, and once you have one, you will never stop using it.

Spiralizer This is a wonderful piece of equipment and the answer to raw pasta. It is a quick and easy tool to turn any root vegetable into curly wurly-looking fettuccine!

Good set of knives These will help improve your cutting technique and can improve the appearance of your raw food dishes.

Chocolate molds These molds are great if you would like to make raw chocolate. You can also use ice cube trays, because any mold will make your inventions more professional.

Ice cream machine This machine is a wonderful indulgence, especially if you like raw ice cream.

Mandolin This is a handy tool for creating even, thin slices of fruits and vegetables. I like to use one if I'm preparing something fancy.

Coffee grinder You only need a small one, but it is so worthwhile because it grinds your nuts and seeds easily. They are also cheap and simple to clean. I use my coffee grinder as much as my food processor.

breakfast

HYDRATING BREAKFAST

Every day has a different quality and the body's needs are different from the day before. Children are also growing physically and expanding mentally, so they might crave something different from the usual bowl of fruit or cereal. Having a good repertoire of staple breakfasts and seeing how your mood takes you is the best approach to happy mornings!

I recommend both adults and children start the day with a good amount of mineral-rich liquid. My favorite options are coconut water, vegetable juice, and green smoothies. These are wonderful at hydrating our cells after a long night of sleeping. I personally keep on liquid fasting until noon because this suits my needs, gives me tons of energy, and there is no wasted time preparing food, but everyone's needs are different. Once you've hydrated, your true need should kick in, whether it be a chunk of raw chocolate or a bowl of granola. Just make sure you start as you mean to go on: meet your needs, not your unhealthy cravings.

Vegetable juices These juices are highly alkaline, hydrating, and packed full of easily absorbable minerals, such as potassium and magnesium. Drinking fresh vegetable juices will also regulate your sugar levels and help to start the day calmly.

Green smoothies These are a blend of leafy greens and fruit, which is an incredibly powerful source of fiber, nutrients, and protein. Blending greens makes their amino acids readily available as a reliable protein source.

Fruit smoothies These are another fantastic alkaline and energy-giving option. Always make sure to add a little hemp, flax, or chia seeds to help slow the release of fruit sugar into the blood. Fruit smoothies are packed full of antioxidants and slow-release carbohydrates.

Soaked sprouts These are a good nourishing, digestible, and grounding breakfast for everyone.

Raw desserts and cakes Yes, these can be a good idea, even for breakfast! The fats and proteins are sometimes just what you need to start the day.

off to the jungle

There is a song I learned as a very young girl at school: "What do you do when you want to go to the loo [bathroom] in an English country garden? Pull down your pants and terrify the ants in an English country garden."

On the first day of our new commune life, this inane ditty is running through my head as I find myself walking through the jungle and suddenly needing the bathroom. A whole new light is now being shed on that song with the realization that the ants here are the stinging and biting kind. They are not likely to be terrified of me. The variety and complexity of nefarious insects is something I really need to learn about.

The only piece of information that has stayed with me from our commune welcome earlier today is that it is scorpion season. Scorpions have seasons? Where I come from, wealthy socialites have seasons . . . Wow, so this is the reality of the deurbanized lifestyle I have been craving all these years.

As we enter our open wooden house—the shack—I am struck by the majestic view up here on the rim of our jungle basin. By day, a paradise without question, but by night, I am imagining a different scenario. The house itself is basic, but beautiful: totally open, front and back, allowing unparalleled views of the jungle and ocean beyond, yet also unimpeded access to nature and all its wonders therein. Looking at the children, they seem calm, convincing me to quash any sense of unease I might have and to start stepping up to the plate. Adaptation is easy I say; now, where do we all sleep? Upstairs is a large bed with an enormous mosquito net, so it looks like we'll be huddled together like a proper jungle family. I take a moment to reflect: insects, suffocating heat, mosquitoes, and the delights of whatever nighttime jungle terrors Mother Nature has in store. Oh and two incredibly jet-lagged children. Help!

Living in a tropical paradise, as it seems I now do, it is essential to make use of the abundant fruits growing virtually on our doorstep. Our current favorite fruits are bananas and mangoes. From the local store, we obtain all the herbs and greens that are harvested in the commune garden, so everything is 100 percent organic. This is just the best smoothie to start the day and a fantastic first food for my ten-month-old, who likes to eat it with a spoon from a jelly jar (always a good shaker in the absence of the right equipment).

TROPICAL DOORSTEP SMOOTHIE

Serves 4 – Preparation time 5 minutes

1 mango, peeled, pitted, and sliced
2 bananas, peeled and chopped
½ cucumber, peeled and coarsely chopped
1 cup spinach or any wild greens available
½ cup fresh mint leaves
1 cup spring or filtered water

Put the mango and bananas into a blender with the remaining ingredients. Blend until really smooth and creamy, adding more water if needed. This smoothie is thick and filling. Pour into glasses and serve.

This incredibly refreshing drink is our typical morning juice because it helps to hydrate and soothe the digestive tract for the day ahead.

MORNING SUN JUICE

Serves 4 - Preparation time 10 minutes

1 large cucumber, coarsely chopped
8 celery stalks, coarsely chopped
4 apples, coarsely chopped
1 cup leafy greens
¼ cup fresh parsley
½-inch piece of fresh ginger, chopped
2 limes or lemons, rind cut away, coarsely chopped
2 beets, coarsely chopped

Put all the ingredients, except the beets, into a juicer. Juice the beets separately; it will give the drink a beautiful two-tone look to it. Pour equal parts of both juices into glasses and serve.

This is our family favorite—a beautifully nutritious and filling breakfast. We used to make it with honey, but dates make it so much more decadent and tasty. Serve with Morning Nut Milk (see page 35) or store-bought nut milk.

APPLE AND DATE
GRANOLA

Serves 12 - Preparation time 20 minutes, plus 2 hours to soak and 12 hours to dehydrate

2 cups almonds, skin on, soaked for 2 hours, then drained
1 cup pecans, soaked for 2 hours, then drained
½ cup pumpkin seeds, soaked for 2 hours, then drained
1 cup sunflower seeds, soaked for 2 hours, then drained
1 cup dried dates, soaked for 20 minutes, then drained
½ cup freshly squeezed orange juice
6 apples, chopped
1 teaspoon ground cinnamon
½ teaspoon sea salt
½ cup dried coconut flakes

Put the dates, orange juice, apples, cinnamon, and salt into a food processor and process until you have a sweet thick paste. Add the nuts and pulse until well chopped, then add the seeds and coconut and pulse a few more times. Scoop the mixture onto 3 Paraflexx sheets, then put the sheets onto dehydrator trays and dehydrate at 120°F for 12 hours. The granola can be stored in an airtight container in the refrigerator for 2 weeks.

Yes, you can have your cake and eat it, too! Cheesecake is wonderful to serve for breakfast, as it is packed full of good fats and a lot of the nourishing B vitamins from the nuts and seeds; sometimes you just want something a little heavier in the morning.

CHEESECAKE FOR BREAKFAST

Serves 8–10 – Preparation time 30 minutes, plus 2 hours to soak and 2 hours to freeze

Start with the crumb crust. Throw the almonds into a food processor and process until coarsely chopped. With the machine still running, gradually add the dates, vanilla, and salt until it forms a sticky mass. Press the mixture into an 8-inch loose-bottom tart pan and place in the freezer to set while you make the filling.

Put all the cream filling ingredients, except the coconut oil, into a blender and blend until smooth and creamy (adding more water, if needed). With the machine still running, slowly pour in the coconut oil. Pour the filling over the crumb crust and place in the freezer to set for 2 hours.

Top with the sliced strawberries and serve. Alternatively, you can freeze the cheesecake for up to 1 week.

Cream filling

2½ cups raw cashew nuts, soaked for 2 hours then drained

½ cup coconut meat (optional)

1 cup spring or filtered water

½ cup agave nectar or raw honey

¾ cup lemon or mango juice (optional, if you want a flavored cheesecake)

1 teaspoon lemon zest

1 teaspoon fresh vanilla bean seeds or 2 teaspoons vanilla extract

a pinch of salt

¼ cup coconut oil

Crumb crust

2½ cups almonds, skin on

1 cup fresh dates

1 teaspoon vanilla extract

a pinch of sea salt

Topping

1 cup strawberries, hulled and sliced

notes on a commune

Yes, we really are living in a commune! Before we left home many months ago, I showed pictures of this place to my mother and she said, "You'll either be running for the hills or you'll never come back." I have to say that after only a couple of weeks, I am already experiencing both these emotions simultaneously. I admit I did enjoy the shock value of telling my London friends that we were selling everything and going to experience different jungle locations in Costa Rica. Most of them looked at me as if to say, "you're mad!" and although I kept assuring them it was a "natural progression," I was without doubt a little nervous. I was very conscious of the fact that this was not just my life, or my husband's; we also have the huge and very tangible responsibility for two very small children.

When I first imagined the design of a commune, I thought it would be basic in structure and probably not efficiently run. This place, however, is very impressive on both of these fronts. My first impression is that the infrastructure is really fantastic; everything is wonderfully designed in both an eco-sustainable and tasteful way to blend into the beautiful jungle environment that surrounds us.

The main hall, which is where the whole community meets for daily yoga and silent sitting (an hour of group-led meditation or "satsang"), is the most impressive of all: a huge domelike building with marble flooring and a stunningly intricate bamboo lattice roof.

The water comes fresh from a spring on the land, is regularly tested to exacting standards, and—because we are so far from any real civilization—is in no need of filtering. I find it both amazing and stunning in simplicity that in Costa Rica, where you're almost forced to drink from plastic bottles, we can drink fresh, clean water straight from a tap.

It's incredible to think how much work goes into the running of the multiplicity of courses and workshops that serve such an important and defining purpose within communal life. The programs are extremely varied, from fairly standard stuff—the likes of yoga and breath work—to programs that most Western world dwellers would regard as a little more "out there." There are tantric courses, meditative courses on awareness, journeys of intense personal discovery, courses on love, on healing, even on discovering your totem animal. I felt quite overwhelmed by my potential to unravel in such a spiritually evolved place. I'm not sure I was ready for that, with two small children to look after. We just wanted a good platform from which to start the rest of our life, not to be put through a healing crisis!

"Is this place going to shake our very existence? Make us question our purpose? Or is it only if you do the program?" I asked the lady in the Welcome Center. "No," she said with a wry smile, "just being part of this place will stir up what needs to come out. Your time here will be more than you possibly imagined!" Wow, okay, hold on kids, this is going to be some ride!

When I'm very busy and need a boost, I make this protein-rich drink, because it is packed full of antioxidant-rich berries and immune-feeding medicinal mushrooms. You can add whatever extra berry yumminess you want.

BERRY CRAZY

Serves 2 - Preparation time 5 minutes

1 cup fresh strawberries, hulled
1 cup fresh raspberries or blueberries
¼ cup goji berries
1 frozen banana
1 tablespoon hulled hemp seeds
1 tablespoon raw honey
1 teaspoon chia seeds (optional but adds thickness)
1 teaspoon medicinal mushrooms (optional)
1 cup spring or filtered water

Put all the ingredients into a blender, and blend until smooth. Pour into glasses and serve.

Medicinal mushrooms People often ask me what are the best immune-boosting herbs, and my top recommendations are medicinal mushrooms. Each medicinal mushroom possesses its own magical properties; however, using a blend of mushrooms really feeds, supports, and works as an insurance system for the immune and nervous systems.

Mushrooms are extremely rich in immune-enhancing polysaccharides (simple plant sugars), which science has proven to be one of the reasons why our immune system responds so well to certain plants and nutrient-rich foods. I am a big fan of reishi and chaga mushrooms, but any mushroom blends are highly beneficial. These particular mushrooms are fabulous immune tonics due to their high potency of antioxidants and polysaccharides that protect against free-radical damage. They also help to strengthen a child's nervous system and are fantastic preventatives—far superior to any synthetic multivitamin. Reishi is also good for a chronic cough and beta glucan-rich chaga can help chronic allergies.

Used over the course of a couple of months, medicinal mushrooms may also have the potential to calm an emotional, highly spirited child. In my opinion, medicinal mushrooms are future foods and are one of the most important, well-researched, and preventative medicines of today.

Hemp seeds One of the most nutrient-rich and delicious food sources on the planet, hulled hemp seeds are packed with protein and are rich in iron, zinc, calcium, and vitamin E. Hemp seeds contain the perfect balance of the essential fatty acids omega-3, -6, and -9. They are key for enriching brain function, beautifying the skin, and enabling the body to create proteins, such as antibodies that ward off infection before symptoms of sickness begin. Hemp is the only edible seed that contains gamma-linolenic acid, the active ingredient also found in evening primrose oil, which is very useful if you experience premenstrual syndrome (PMS). Hemp also contains nutrients that help to aid detoxification.

The hemp plant is even good for the planet. It will grow almost anywhere with no need for pesticides or fertilizers, and its presence is beneficial for both the soil and the atmosphere, making it one of the most ethical and sustainable plants in existence.

Hemp is a great food to pack when traveling because it works wonderfully as a base for smoothies, is great sprinkled on practically any fruit (especially bananas), and gives an added protein kick to all meals.

This creamy and delicious shake is wonderfully filling and at the same time cleansing because of the cilantro, which is a fantastic heavy metal detoxifier. The combination of the protein-digesting enzyme bromelian from the pineapple and the fatty acids from the coconut butter helps to boost the metabolism. This is my favorite fruit-base smoothie, and it leaves me really satisfied!

DETOX
PINEAPPLE
SHAKE

Serves 2 - Preparation time 5 minutes

½ pineapple, peeled and chopped

1 frozen banana

1 cucumber, peeled and coarsely chopped

1 teaspoon fresh cilantro leaves

1 teaspoon coconut butter

1 tablespoon hulled hemp seeds

pinch of chopped fresh chile
(depending on how spicy you like it)

1 teaspoon raw honey

1 teaspoon fresh vanilla bean seeds or
2 teaspoons vanilla extract

1 cup spring or filtered water

Put all the ingredients into a blender and blend well until smooth. Pour the shake into glasses and drink immediately.

breakfast

This breakfast has been a staple of our family for years. Buckwheat is a magnesium-, calcium-, and protein-rich grain, and combined with essential fats and antioxidant-rich lucuma and cacao powder, this is just the best-ever breakfast and feeds two hungry kids.

BEST-EVER
BUCKWHEAT
CEREAL

Serves 2 - Preparation time 10 minutes, plus 20 minutes to soak

2 cups raw buckwheat, soaked for 20 minutes then drained and well rinsed

¼ cup flaxseed oil

2 tablespoons any raw nut butter

1 tablespoon lucuma powder

1 tablespoon raw cacao powder

1 teaspoon raw honey or natural sweetener

2 cups ice-cold almond milk, to serve (optional)

Mix the flaxseed oil and nut butter together to form a runny paste, then stir in the lucuma powder, cacao powder, and honey to thicken. Add the rinsed buckwheat and mix together. Eat on its own or add some ice-cold almond milk.

intuitive eating

Today, I heard an amazing quote, "the subtle energy of what you eat becomes your mind," which I discovered is from "The Upanishads," a sacred text of the Hindu religion. This has really struck me and makes me feel so blessed and fortunate that most of the time my mind and body naturally gravitate toward the most alive and nutritious foods.

People who know how much raw food I eat always say to me, "but it's so hard, how do you stick to it?" I have realized that it's not about "sticking to it;" it's just intuitively what my body wants to do, and I believe that it is at this stage we start to improve our health. I am always on a mission to feel as fantastic and energized as I can, and eating this way simply checks those boxes. The really exciting thing is that once you include raw foods, nutrient-rich foods, and herbs in your diet, your taste buds gradually change: the cravings for cooked food or junk food stop, and the cravings for the healthier foods start. Most importantly, you hone your instinctive skills in understanding what your body wants you to eat.

I believe that when it comes to children you have to give them space to find their own intuitive eating path. I am a great believer in providing them with the best choices and then allowing them to create their own concoctions. Obviously there is not always the time to do this, and it can be a messy affair, but it is an investment in your child's future. It really helps you discover what their palate desires rather than guessing at what they would like. If you start when they are just old enough to be able to feed themselves, they soon learn what they like and how they like it.

This is my daughter Zella's favorite raw breakfast. She decided chocolate and bananas tasted good together, so we then made this yummy cashew cream to go with them. It is a perfect example of what children can come up with when they are given a positive choice of what to eat.

CREAMY
BANANA
CHOCOLATE BREAKFAST

Serves 2 - Preparation time 5 minutes, plus 4 hours to soak

Cashew cream
2 cups raw cashew nuts, soaked for 4 hours then drained
½ cup spring or filtered water
juice of 2 lemons
1 vanilla bean, split lengthwise and seeds scraped out
2 tablespoons agave nectar or natural sweetener

Banana breakfast
2 bananas, peeled and chopped
2 tablespoons cashew cream (see above)
juice of ½ orange
1 tablespoon raw carob powder or raw cacao powder

To make the cashew cream, put the cashew nuts, water, lemon juice, vanilla seeds, and agave nectar into a blender and blend until smooth.

Put the chopped bananas into a bowl, add the cashew cream, orange juice, and carob powder, and stir together until combined. Serve. Although I make this for Zella's breakfast, I must admit that I often hold a little back to snack on… it's wonderful as a midnight feast.

Making fresh nut milk is a staple in our household. It replaces pasteurized dairy products and is significantly more nutritious.

MORNING NUT MILK

Makes 3 cups
Preparation time 10 minutes, plus 8 hours to soak

1 cup almonds or brazil nuts or hazelnuts, soaked for 8 hours then drained and rinsed

1 tablespoon raw honey or natural sweetener

1 teaspoon vanilla extract

a pinch of sea salt

4 cups spring or filtered water

Put all the ingredients into a blender and blend for up to 1 minute, until the nuts are processed and very finely ground. Pour the mixture through a nut milk bag for a smooth and pulp-free consistency. Alternatively, pour through a fine strainer a couple of times until smooth. You can store it in the refrigerator for 3 days.

This is a little gem that I invented when a hardcore coffee-drinking friend came to stay. It is not only yummy but will also give you tons of energy!

RAW ICED MOCHACHINO

Serves 2 - Preparation time 5 minutes

1 cup nut milk (see opposite) or spring or filtered water for a less creamy texture

1 teaspoon mucuna powder

1 teaspoon mesquite

1 tablespoon raw cacao powder

1 tablespoon raw honey or natural sweetener

6 ice cubes

Put the nut milk into a blender and add the remaining ingredients, except ice. Blend until smooth, then add the ice cubes and pulse for 10 seconds to produce a crunchy consistency. Pour into glasses and serve.

Mucuna powder Traditionally, mucuna has been used as an aphrodisiac due to its high dopamine-inducing properties, so it can also help people with Parkinson's disease. This nutrient-rich bean is great at restoring the adrenal systems of people who have been big coffee drinkers. Add it to smoothies and all forms of chocolate, beginning with ⅛ teaspoon, then slowly increasing to ½ teaspoon or more.

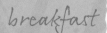

This was inspired by my trips to Asia and the wonderful blend of fruit and spices used in recipes there. In the jungle, where there's such an abundance of fresh fruit on my doorstep, it's difficult not to crave this! This is a gorgeously flavorsome and filling way to start the day.

MANGO LASSI
MOUSSE
WITH BERRIES

Serves 2 - Preparation time 5 minutes, plus 10 minutes to soak

10 raw cashew nuts, soaked for 10 minutes then drained
2 mangoes, peeled, pitted, and sliced
1 frozen banana
¼ teaspoon ground cardamom
¼ star anise
2 tablespoons nut milk or spring or filtered water
1 teaspoon coconut butter
1 teaspoon chia seeds
1 cup berries

Put the cashew nuts into a blender with the sliced mango, banana, spices, nut milk, cashew nuts, coconut butter, and chia seeds and blend until you achieve a smooth almost creamy consistency, adding a little more water, if necessary. Pour the mixture into a beautiful bowl and throw on the berries. If you prefer, omit the spices and just make a fruity bowl of goodness.

This drink is simply delicious! It is a thick, rich protein shake with a mellow maca boost. It provides a great source of omega-3 and will fill you up until lunchtime!

POUR DOWN THE PINK
PROTEIN

Serves 2 - Preparation time 5 minutes

1 large scoop Sunwarrior protein powder or a hemp protein powder
1 cup frozen berries or 1 frozen banana
1 tablespoon chia seeds
1 tablespoon coconut butter
1 tablespoon raw honey or natural sweetener
1 teaspoon maca powder
1½ cups spring or filtered water

Put all the ingredients into a blender and blend together for a quick 10 seconds. Pour into glasses and serve immediately.

Coconut oil Coconut oil has antibacterial, antiviral, and antifungal properties. It also increases the absorption of omega-3, so is very useful if taken alongside flax and chia seeds. Combined with cacao butter, coconut oil also helps to prevent and fade stretch marks.

PROTEIN FOR LUNCH

Lunchtime can be anything from a large smoothie to a colorful salad; however, wherever I am in the world, I always try and make sure that lunch is a protein-rich meal, so an addition of hemp seeds, seaweeds, avocado, nuts, and seeds is always a good idea. Our bodies are happier receiving protein at this time of day, when our digestive systems are usually at their strongest. Eating protein also stops us from having mid-afternoon dips in energy. This is also a good time for the body to digest a lot of raw salad, so stock up on greens.

People ask me how they should prepare for a lunch on the go. I always advise traveling with a good amount of raw or wheat-free crackers, an avocado, and some kind of dip; this ensures that you have a protein-rich, easy-to-prepare lunch or snack. Salads are easy to carry around; just make a separately prepared dressing to pour on later.

Salads Eating big leafy green salads will ensure you stock up on extra minerals, vitamins, and fiber. To fill you up even more, add additional protein in the form of antioxidant- and essential fatty acid-rich foods, such as goji berries, hemp seeds, olives, or raw cheeses.

Protein fillers Make protein-rich smoothies with leafy greens, hemp seeds, or brown rice; these liquid meals will keep you going for hours.

Crackers Make these with energy-giving, vitamin B-rich nuts and seeds to fill you up.

Sandwiches Stuff seed-made breads with enzyme-rich sprouts, raw vegetables, and other alkaline salad greens for a truly filling meal.

settling in

Without doubt, the first few weeks here have been challenging. Djuna has been up most nights teething, so I feel like a zombie, and Jamie is enduring a process of personality deconstruction with a curious blend of steely abandon (he has enrolled in a "Transformation Program" to help place him more in the moment and eliminate his ego and judgment). Meanwhile, little Zella, who was terrifically excited about the prospect of going to a new school and meeting new friends, has found the reality of it all a little too much for her sensitive little soul. After all, we plucked her out of her familiar and comfortable routine in London and took her away from her friends, and off around the world. While I'm certain, both intuitively and intellectually, that this kind of experience for a young child is positive, I'm sure the reality of it is daunting. We are also struggling a little with our purpose. What are we doing here? What do we do after this?

We have found talking to people and sharing our inner struggles a fabulous way to tune in and make sense of it all, so the lunchtime ritual here has become a treasured part of the day. The whole commune gathers together to enjoy the wonderful foods provided by the hard work of the collective and the surrounding gifts of nature. It's been a chance to sample some fabulous homemade foods; our diet now is a blend of vegan, veggie, and raw, with an emphasis on eating according to the seasons and, of course, nutrient-rich foods, which in my opinion is the optimum way to eat!

Lunch is also symbolically important because many in the Ayurvedic traditions regard it as the most important meal of the day, primarily due to one's digestion functioning optimally at this time. Lunch here, therefore, has an almost celebratory feel to it.

This is my favorite lunchtime salad. If we are not somewhere that's growing tropical fruits, then I just replace them with citrus fruits, such as oranges, grapefruit, or clementines.

TROPICAL SALAD OF LOVE

Serves 2 - Preparation time 15 minutes

Salad
4 large handfuls of lettuce or mixed greens
1 avocado, peeled, pitted, and chopped
1 tomato, chopped
1 cucumber, peeled and julienned
2 tablespoons hulled hemp seeds
a handful of torn dulse
**1 mango or papaya, peeled, pitted, and chopped
(reserve the mango skin for the dressing)**
2 teaspoons raw cheese (optional)

Citrus dressing
3 tablespoons olive oil
juice of 1 lemon
1 tablespoon apple cider vinegar
squeezed juice from the mango skin

Put all the ingredients for the salad into a large bowl. To make the dressing, put all the ingredients into a small bowl and mix together, then pour over the salad, toss until coated, then serve.

This is a great recipe to get all the family to eat lettuce; the nut butter, bananas, and cacao combination always wins everyone over. It is perfect to serve for lunch or even at any time of the day!

HEMPY BURRITOS

Serves 2 - Preparation time 10 minutes

2 tablespoons nut butter
2 Boston or other butterhead lettuce, leaves separated
2 bananas, peeled and chopped
1 avocado, peeled, pitted, and chopped
2 tablespoons hulled hemp seeds
2 teaspoons raw cacao nibs

Spread the nut butter onto the lettuce, then add the chopped bananas and avocado. Sprinkle the hemp seeds and raw cacao nibs over the top to finish, fold into little bundles, and serve.

This is another burrito favorite. It's very filling and I love the sweetness of the fruit compared to the Hempy Burritos, which are savory! Mango and tomato actually help support digestion, so they are good to eat in combination.

MANGO, AVOCADO, AND TOMATO BURRITOS

Serves 2 - Preparation time 10 minutes

1 mango, peeled, pitted, and chopped
2 tomatoes, chopped
1 avocado, peeled, pitted, and chopped
2 tablespoons olive oil
1 teaspoon apple cider vinegar
a pinch of salt
a handful of dulse (optional)
4 large romaine lettuce leaves

Put all the ingredients, except the lettuce leaves, into a bowl and mix well to combine. Spoon the mixture into the lettuce leaves, fold into little bundles, and serve. It's a little messy so use a plate.

Sea vegetables are a great addition to your daily diet: both the iodine and trace minerals found in this delicious food have huge all-round health benefits, including proper weight management, correct absorption of vitamins and minerals, protection against radiation, and hormonal health. Seaweed is also a protein-rich food. Arame and dulse are the mildest of all the seaweeds and are the perfect way to introduce people to eating sea vegetables.

SUPER SEAWEED SALAD

Serves 2 - Preparation time 20 minutes, plus 5 minutes to soak

Salad

a handful of arame, soaked for 5 minutes then drained and patted dry

½ cup carrot, julienned

½ cup cucumber, peeled and julienned

1 cup raw corn kernels

1 cup lentil sprouts

a handful of dulse, torn

Dressing

2 tablespoons tahini

1 teaspoon ginger juice (piece of fresh ginger juiced in the juicer)

1 tablespoon lemon juice

1 tablespoon raw honey

¼ cup raw sesame oil

To make the salad, put the arame, carrot and cucumber julienne, corn kernels, and sprouts into a large bowl and mix together to combine. Sprinkle the dulse on top.

For the dressing, put the tahini into a large bowl and whisk in the ginger juice, lemon juice, honey, and sesame oil until you have a paste-like dressing.

Pour the dressing over the salad, and enjoy!

This is a great bread to make a lot of if you have a dehydrator. My favorite sandwich is a DLT—Dulse, Lettuce, and Tomato. Layer your bread with avocado, sliced tomato, dulse, and plenty of hemp or olive oil and balsamic vinegar—yummy and filling!

PROTEIN-RICH
SANDWICH BREAD

Makes 12 slices - Preparation time 25 minutes, plus 10 minutes to soak and 8–12 hours to dehydrate

2 cups sunflower seeds, soaked for 10 minutes, then drained
1 cup hulled hemp seeds
2 cups fresh carrot juice
1 tablespoon olive oil
1 tablespoon fresh parsley
1 teaspoon raw honey
2 cups ground flaxseeds

Put all the ingredients, except the ground flaxseeds, into a food processor and process until the mixture is almost a paste. Stir in the flaxseeds.

Spread the mixture onto 3 Paraflexx sheets then score to create 12 slices. Put the sheets onto dehydrator trays and dehydrate at 115°F for 4–6 hours. Flip the mixture over and dehydrate for an additional 4–6 hours, until dry. Cut into 12 slices.

You can store the bread in an airtight container for up to 5 days.

school lunches

Zella has just started a new school, where she has to bring in her own lunch. I was immediately nervous, because I knew the other children would probably be eating foods that I choose not to give Zella. However, she is now four years old and understands a great deal about eating for energy, so instead of sending her off with a gluten- and sugar-laden lunch box, we come up with our own ideas and have even invented a few of our own snack bars (see pages 71 and 78).

This is what Zella's lunch box currently consists of:

- 1 container of chopped fruit (mango, pineapple, or apple)
- 1 container of raw vegetables (celery, cucumber, and carrot)
- 4 raw crackers (usually flax and almond) or raw pizza slices
- 1 container of raw dip (usually a cashew nut or herbed sunflower pâté)
- 1 snack bar or cookie (see page 51)
- 1 container of mixed nuts and goji berries
- 1 small container of dairy-free fruit yogurt

Kids love these savory but slightly sweet crackers. It is a family staple! Serve these with Red Cashew Cheese Dip (see page 104) for a very healthy lunch.

KIDS GO
CRACKERS

Makes 24 - Preparation time 15 minutes, plus 12 hours to dehydrate

- 1 cup ground flaxseeds
- 1 cup whole flaxseeds
- 1 cup sunflower seeds
- 1 cup carrot pulp (leftover juice pulp)
- 1 cup orange, apple, or mango juice
- 1 tablespoon tamari
- 1 tablespoon dulse flakes (optional)
- ½ teaspoon sea salt

Put all the ingredients into a food processor and process until smooth. Turn the mixture out onto a Paraflexx sheet and press into a large square. With a knife or spatula, score the mixture into the size crackers you would like.

Put the sheets onto a dehydrator tray and dehydrate at 125°F overnight. As soon as this side is dry, flip them over and dehydrate for an additional 4 hours, until dry. They should take about 12 hours in total to dehydrate.

This is another great super-healthy snack for kids' lunch boxes. We make them in bulk because Zella's friends always ask her to share them at snack time. They look like the real deal, but taste oh so much nicer!

RAW CHOCOLATE CHIP
NUTRIENT-RICH
COOKIES

Makes 36 - Preparation time 30 minutes, plus 16 hours to dehydrate

- 4 cups dry raw cashew nuts
- 1 cup cashew butter
- ¼ cup dried dates
- 1 tablespoon maca powder
- ½ cup raw honey
- 2 tablespoons cacao nibs or raw chocolate pieces
- 1 teaspoon sea salt

Put the cashew nuts into a blender or coffee grinder and grind them into a fine flour. Add the ground nuts to a food processor together with the remaining ingredients and process until you achieve a sticky, doughy mass.

Roll the dough into a ball, then place between 2 dehydrator sheets and use a rolling pin to roll the dough into a ½-inch-thick pastry. Use a cookie cutter to cut out 36 pretty shapes and place them onto several Paraflexx sheets with a spatula.

Put the sheets onto dehydrator trays and dehydrate at 120°F for 12 hours. Flip the cookies over and dry for an additional 4 hours, or until crunchy.

This is a rich treat, made creamy by the use of avocado, fruit, and nut milk. It is a wonderful substitute for dairy, so it's great for those who are lactose intolerant or who want to reduce their dairy intake. You can make your own nut milk or buy a range of them at your local health food store.

DAIRY-FREE FRUIT YOGURT

Serves 2 - Preparation time 5 minutes, plus 10 minutes to soak (optional)

1 teaspoon goji berries, soaked for 10 minutes (optional)

1 cup strawberries, chopped pineapple, or mango

1 frozen banana, chopped

1 tablespoon avocado flesh

¼ cup Morning Nut Milk (see page 35), or other nut milk

Put all the ingredients into a blender and blend for 1–2 minutes. If you like to have pieces of strawberry in your yogurt, then blend for a little less time until you achieve the right consistency. Serve.

Goji berries Goji fruit, from the plant Lycium barbarum, is revered in Asia for its youth-preserving, health-protective, strengthening and mood-elevating properties. It has been considered to be a "magical" longevity superfood since the dawn of Asian civilization. This protein-rich berry has four times the amount of antioxidants found in blueberries, contains more beta-carotene (a source of vitamin A) than carrots, and gives you 2mg of iron per handful. They are also another polysaccharide-rich food, so they are extremely beneficial for the immune system.

Goji berries are one of the main fruit used in China's amazing herbal system and are regarded as one of the elite tonic fruit in the world. They are one of the best and most delicious strengthening fruits for children, and I would always advise parents to give them instead of raisins, because they offer superior nutrition. They are great soaked for a couple of hours and added to all kinds of different smoothies—with a medicinal punch if accompanied by hemp seeds, chaga mushrooms, and cacao.

I really recommend doing your research and sourcing only the very best organic plump goji berries.

Sprouting grains is a fantastic way to access their full potential and increase their nutritional profile. Quinoa, as well as being extremely nutrient dense, has prebiotic properties, feeding the beneficial bacteria in your digestive tract.

QUINOA SPROUTS, AVOCADO, AND TOMATO MARINARA WRAPS

Serves 4 - Preparation time 10 minutes, plus 32 hours to sprout

2 cups quinoa, sprouted (see below)
1 cup Tomato Marinara Sauce (see page 86)
8 romaine or butterhead lettuce leaves ('boats')
2 avocados, peeled, pitted, and chopped

Soak the quinoa in a bowl of cold water overnight, then drain and rinse in a colander, strainer, or nut milk bag under cold running water. Let the quinoa stand in the colander, strainer, or nut milk bag for 24 hours, then drain and rinse 3–4 times, until you see little tails beginning to sprout.

When ready to serve, put the quinoa into a large bowl, add the marinara sauce, and mix together. Spoon the quinoa mixture into the lettuce boats and top with chopped avocado to serve. This is a perfect protein-rich lunch.

This is a deliciously soothing and light soup, packed full of minerals, and it is hugely hydrating.

CUCUMBER AND MINT
SUMMER SOUP

Serves 2 - Preparation time 15 minutes, plus 30 minutes to chill (optional)

4 romaine lettuce leaves
1 cucumber, peeled and juiced
1 teaspoon chopped fresh mint
½ cup spring or filtered water
½ teaspoon salt
1 garlic clove
½ ripe avocado, peeled, pitted, and chopped
1 tablespoon olive oil
freshly ground black pepper
ice cubes, to serve (optional)

Put the lettuce, cucumber, mint, water, salt, and garlic into a blender and blend until smooth. While the machine is still running, add the avocado and olive oil through the feeder tube and process until everything is blended. Add more mint, if desired, and season with a little black pepper.

This soup is wonderful served chilled, so either blend again with a couple of ice cubes or place in the refrigerator for 30 minutes, then serve.

I love to nourish myself with this magnesium-rich smoothie. It is packed full of everything you need to stay green and clean.

MAGNESIUM
LUNCH CRUNCH
SMOOTHIE

Serves 2 – Preparation time 5 minutes

¼ ripe avocado, peeled, and pitted
a handful of leafy greens
1 frozen banana
10 frozen or fresh strawberries
1 teaspoon hulled hemp seeds
1 teaspoon raw honey
5 chlorella pills
½ cucumber, peeled and coarsely chopped
1 tablespoon raw cacao nibs
1 cup spring or filtered water

Put all the ingredients into a blender and blend until smooth. Pour into glasses and serve.

Magnesium Our cells are dependent on a good dosage of this supermineral because it is essential for the proper functioning of all the systems of the body. It specifically strengthens and supports the heart muscle, increases brain power, increases flexibility, is imperative to the building of strong bones, and is crucial for a robust immune system.

When the body is deficient in magnesium, things begin to go very wrong—this can leave us open not just to degenerative disease, but also to damage from radiation and heavy metals. Without magnesium, the body accumulates toxins and acid residues and ages rapidly. If you think you might be suffering from magnesium deficiency, I suggest you supplement with ionic magnesium or use magnesium oil topically along with B6, which increases the cellular absorption of magnesium. You can also supplement your diet with B6-rich nutrient-rich foods, such as goji berries, spirulina, and bee pollen.

There are loads of foods that contain magnesium, but the most magnesium-rich ones include leafy green vegetables, especially spinach, chlorella, avocado, oats, raw chocolate, almonds, cashew nuts, and sunflower seeds.

snacks
&
treats

SNACKS & TREATS

These snacks and treats are goodies that fit the bill perfectly whether you're needing something to eat on the go or are just looking for a quick-and-easy meal. Some of these snacks need dehydration, but once you take time to prepare them, you'll be stocked up with treats that you can take with you at a moment's notice. After munching on these raw snacks, you'll feel full and energized, so post-sugar dips will be no more.

I suggest squeezing as many nutrient-rich foods into snacktime as possible, because these foods leave you satisfied but also supply minerals and vitamins. My favorites are protein-rich chlorella and antioxidant-rich goji berries. Raw chocolate also features heavily here because raw cacao is a great mental sharpener due to its natural mood boosters, theobromine and anandamide; it will keep you supercharged until your next meal.

Nut and seed bars These are full of healthy fats and the B vitamins to maintain a healthy nervous system.

Raw chocolate This is mood enhancing and energy giving. Not only is raw cacao a great mental sharpener, but it has also been shown to reduce appetite and allow serotonin to circulate your brain, giving you a relaxed and happy feeling.

Raw vegetables and fruit These feed your body with natural sugars and keep it hydrated and more alkaline, so you feel more energized.

Small salads Handfuls of greens and fruit give you a quick pick-me-up.

Power smoothies Nutrient-rich drinks will leave you feeling satisfied until your next meal.

chocolate smiles

This week we have all turned a significant corner. Djuna is sleeping better, while Zella is becoming more settled in her commune school and seems to have finally accepted this place as our home. I have a sneaky feeling that the reason for this turnaround is due to the extremely high-quality chocolate and nutrient-rich smoothies she is consuming. She has even taken to dancing around, declaring, "I love living here!"

When school finishes at lunchtime each day, all the kids get a coconut cacao ice cream from the Wild Treats Bar, which I think is one of the best things about living here. The bar is a little shack in the jungle that creates delicious and healthy snacks, mostly made from local produce and nutrient-rich foods. Raw chocolate can be a little stimulating, but in small amounts and on occasion, it is heart-opening, energy-giving, and puts a big smile on your face. It also seems completely normal to be consuming this complex and nutrient-dense food in a place where it's indigenous. It is a little like going back in time, because here in the commune they are so obsessed with their chocolate that even the commune currency (the only currency permitted for purchases) is "chocos." One choco equals one dollar, and little cards represent a variety of different units of chocos. This is reminiscent of the Mayan method, where they literally would swap cacao beans for food. A rabbit was worth 30 cacao beans, an avocado 3 cacao beans, and a good turkey was worth as much as 100 cacao beans. I have taken to wondering: how much for a husband?

To supplement the pervasiveness of this chocolate culture, everyone at the commune appears to do at least a daily cacao shot. I honor the chocolate god, whoever you are, for now I have a little girl who is happy!

This is a little dose of "natural pick-me-up" and might just be the answer to those espresso shots you are trying to give up! I love to have a carafe of this yummy drink in my refrigerator so I can swig from it whenever I need a boost.

CACAO SHOT MIX

Serves 4 – Preparation time 5 minutes

½ cup raw cashew nuts

1 cup spring or filtered water

1 tablespoon raw cacao nibs or beans

1 tablespoon raw cacao powder

2 tablespoons raw honey, agave nectar, or yacon syrup

½ teaspoon fresh vanilla bean seeds or 1 teaspoon vanilla extract (optional)

1 teaspoon coconut butter (for a slightly creamier taste)

a pinch of ground cinnamon

a pinch of cayenne pepper

Put all the ingredients into a blender and blend for at least 1 minute, until you have a fairly thick and intense chocolate drink.

Pour into glasses and serve. Only do a maximum of 2 shots per day, otherwise you might feel a little wired!

This is a little invention we came up with when we wanted to re-create our friend Adi's delicious chocolate balls. This recipe is a vitamin-B and magnesium explosion, to which you can also add nutrient-rich herbs or additional ground nuts and seeds.

ZELLA'S BEST CHOCOLATE
ORANGE BALLS

Makes 10 large and 14 small –
Preparation time 20 minutes, plus 4 minutes to cool and freeze

1 cup cacao butter

½ cup raw cacao powder

½ cup lucuma powder

1 tablespoon maca powder

1 teaspoon vanilla extract

8 drops of orange essential oil

¼ teaspoon sea salt

2 tablespoons raw honey or natural sweetener

½ cup sunflower seeds

½ cup organic oats

¼ cup hulled hemp seeds (optional)

¼ cup chopped or ground pumpkin seeds

2 tablespoons buckwheaties, optional (already sprouted and dehydrated buckwheat)

½ cup coconut flakes or ground almonds

Slowly melt the cacao butter in a double boiler or in a heatproof bowl set over a saucepan of gently simmering water. When the butter has melted, transfer to a bowl, add the next seven ingredients, and stir until it is a smooth chocolate consistency, adding more sweetener, if you prefer. Let the cacao butter mixture cool slightly, for about 2 minutes, then stir in the remaining ingredients, except the coconut flakes or ground almonds. Freeze the chocolate mixture for 2 minutes.

Use a teaspoon to scoop out sticky mounds, roll them into balls, then roll in the coconut flakes or ground almonds until coated. Serve.

Maca Also known as "Peruvian ginseng," maca is a nutrient-packed root vegetable that grows in the mountain plateaus of the Peruvian Andes. Maca is rich in amino acids, phytonutrients, vitamins, and minerals, and has been used as a traditional source of both food and medicine by indigenous people since the time of the Incas. My experience with maca, both personally and clinically, has shown me its ability to quickly increase energy, stamina, and endurance; enhance libido; support the immune system and adrenal function; reduce chronic fatigue; and regulate and support the endocrine system. It is also a great tonic for men to improve and increase sperm count.

Maca is a powerful adaptogen, meaning that it adapts to the body's needs. As a food, the dried root is sweet and pungent, and when blended with water, it has a creamy almost malty flavor. Maca is a warming herb, so it is excellent when eaten in cold climates.

Maca is perfect to add to a supergreen drink, or a protein smoothie, or used as an ingredient in raw bars or cooked cakes or muffins. I suggest starting by adding 1 teaspoon of maca powder to your diet a day over the course of a month, building up to 1 tablespoon.

I love making power-packed chocolate; it just means you can add whatever goodies you have in your cupboard or refrigerator, and it makes a great little therapeutic snack.

CRUNCHY CHOCOLATE HEARTS

Makes 20 - Preparation time 20 minutes, plus 3 hours to set

1 cup cacao butter
½ cup raw cacao powder
½ cup lucuma powder
1 tablespoon maca powder
1 teaspoon mucuna powder
1 tablespoon raw honey
1 tablespoon hulled hemp seeds
1 tablespoon buckwheaties (already sprouted and dehydrated buckwheat)
1 tablespoon goji berries

Slowly melt the cacao butter in a double boiler or in a heatproof bowl set over a saucepan of gently simmering water. When the butter has melted, add the powders and honey and stir until it is a smooth chocolate consistency. Stir in the hemp seeds, buckwheaties, and goji berries.

Pour the mixture into heart-shaped molds and let set at room temperature for 3 hours. When set, chill in the refrigerator until ready to serve.

Raw cacao Cacao is an incredibly power-packed food with extremely high amounts of antioxidants and important minerals, such as magnesium and phosphorous. I do, however, recommend that you treat raw chocolate with a great deal of respect. It's designed to be enjoyed in small amounts or used medicinally. Cacao contains theobromine, which dilates the blood vessels, so using cacao as an "envoy" for herbs and nutrient-rich foods to be carried into the body is a demonstration of chocolate put to its proper use.

It is important to be discerning when sourcing your raw chocolate. You really want to do your research and find cacao that is organic and preferably harvested from cacao trees and not cacao bushes. It is also good to be cautious with dosage when feeding to young children. We love it, but are always aware of its medicinal magic, its shamanic folklore, and, of course, its intensity, so treat it with respect and a little bit of awe!

All kids and adults love these crunchy decadent cookies. I recommend that you make them on the small side, because they will fly off the plate!

ALMOND CRUNCH COOKIES

Makes 24 cookies - Preparation time 30 minutes, plus 16 hours to dehydrate

- 2 cups almond nut butter
- 4 cups ground almonds or finely ground almonds
- ½ cup maple syrup
- ½ cup raw honey
- 1 teaspoon sea salt

Put all the ingredients into a food processor and process until you achieve a pastry-like dough. Place the dough between 2 Paraflexx sheets and roll out until it's about ½-inch thick. Cut out 24 shapes, using any shape of cookie cutters you like, then place the cookies onto 2 clean Paraflexx sheets with a spatula.

Put the sheets onto dehydrator trays and dehydrate at 120°F for 6 hours. Flip the cookies over and dehydrate for an additional 10 or so hours. You can dehydrate them for less time, depending on how much crunch you like.

I thank the wonderful Kate Magic for her inspiration for these gorgeous little treats. Kate is one of the UK's leading raw food educators and has been inspiring me for years with her psychedelic recipes.

FLAX HEMP BARS

Makes 16 - Preparation time 20 minutes, plus 1 hour to soak and 18 hours to dehydrate

- 3 cups raw oats (or organic oats)
- 2 tablespoons hulled hemp seeds, soaked for 1 hour then drained
- 1 tablespoon ground flaxseeds, soaked for 1 hour then drained
- ½ cup olive oil
- ½ cup maple syrup
- a pinch of salt
- 1 tablespoon maca powder
- ½ cup lucuma powder
- 1 cup raisins

Put soaked and drained oats and hemp seeds into a food processor with all the remaining ingredients and process until you have a sticky dough.

Spread the dough onto a Paraflexx sheet in a square—it should almost fill 1 sheet—then put the sheet into a dehydrator tray and dehydrate at 120°F for 12 hours. Score into bars with a knife, 2 across by 8 down. Flip them over so they dry evenly on both sides and dry for an additional 6 hours. When they're done, they should be soft, crumbly, and delicious.

This is a great soothing snack for hungry little stomachs. You can use other melons, such as cantaloupe or honeydew if you prefer, and why not try adding a mixture of red and green grapes to the skewers?

CHOCOLATE TROPICAL KEBAB STICKS

Makes 8 skewers or more - Preparation time 15 minutes

5 mangos, peeled and pitted
2 watermelons, peeled and seeded
3 cucumbers, peeled
1 big bag of seedless grapes
raw cacao or carob powder, for sprinkling

Slice and dice all the fruit into cubes. Thread onto 8 skewers and place on a large serving plate. Lightly sprinkle raw cacao or carob powder over the top to finish.

This easy ice cream tastes so rich and creamy you won't believe it's dairy-free! You can double the recipe to serve four to eight people, if you prefer.

RAW VANILLA
ICE CREAM

Serves 2–4 – Preparation time 15 minutes, plus 2 hours to soak, 2 hours to chill, and 4 hours to freeze

- **1 cup raw cashew nuts, soaked for at least 2 hours then drained**
- **1½ cups spring or filtered water**
- **⅓ cup maple syrup**
- **¼ teaspoon salt**
- **1 tablespoon lucuma powder (optional, but works well)**
- **2 teaspoons vanilla extract**
- **½ teaspoon fresh vanilla bean seeds**
- **2 tablespoons cacao butter, melted**

Put all of the ingredients, except the cacao butter, into a blender and blend until you achieve a fairly smooth consistency. While the machine is still running pour the cacao butter through the feeder tube until combined.

Put the mixture into a freezerproof container and chill in the refrigerator for 2 hours, then either place in the freezer for 4 hours to set or churn in an ice cream machine, according to the manufacturer's directions.

Zella's birthday

We have been living here for only two months but have already attended six birthday parties. This has been good and bad! Zella loves the idea of a children's party, and it's great for her to be making new friends. However, things tend to go downhill after an hour of arriving. "Where's the cake, Mama?" "I want those presents—can I have one?" Etc., etc., sound familiar? Also there is, of course, the issue of sugar! I am all for Zella indulging in a little party poison, and I don't like to demonize anything too much, but only in small amounts. Too much sugar drives my little one nuts and, for those who aren't aware, it takes only one teaspoon of the stuff to significantly suppress the immune system for twenty-four hours.

I suppose I assumed that these mindful folk would choose only natural ingredients to give to their children, even on their birthdays, but I then reminded myself of some kids' birthday parties in London, where I had to make a few prompt excuses for our almost immediate departure after seeing some of the brightly colored and not particularly additive-free food on the party table. However, here in the jungle all was good with an abundance of naturally sweetened treats.

Now, looming on the horizon is Zella's own birthday, and the nerves are already setting in. "Are we having a princess birthday, Mama?" "Will all my friends come and bring me presents?" "The cake," said Zella, "can it be a cooked one?"—her third birthday had been a completely raw occasion and I think the cake was more about me projecting what I wanted instead of what was comfortable for her young palate. "Of course, darling." Pause.

"You can do a raw one as well, if you like," said Zella.

Okay, I thought, I get the message. Well, her birthday came and went, and all was peachy. Zella ushered words of thanks whenever gifted with anything: princess dresses, cooked and raw cakes, which were both loved and both eaten.

FULL SPECTRUM CHOCOLATE BIRTHDAY CAKE

This, funnily enough, is now Zella's favorite cake; I think maybe her palate and my raw food creations have become a little more sophisticated over the last year.

Serves 10 - Preparation time 45 minutes, plus 2 hours to soak, and 2 hours to freeze

Milk mousse layer

2 cups raw cashew nuts, soaked for at least 2 hours then drained

½ cup coconut oil

½ cup raw cacao powder

½ cup spring or filtered water

a pinch of sea salt

½ cup maple syrup

2 teaspoons vanilla extract

Chocolate crust

1½ cups pecan nuts

¼ cup buckwheaties (already sprouted and dehydrated buckwheat)

½ cup dried dates

½ cup raw cacao powder

1 teaspoon vanilla extract

a pinch of sea salt

Chocolate frosting

⅓ cup coconut butter

1 teaspoon vanilla extract

3 tablespoons agave nectar

2 tablespoons raw cacao powder

1 tablespoon lucuma powder

For the chocolate crust, put all the ingredients into a food processor and process until the mixture starts to stick together. Press the mixture into a 9-inch springform cake pan.

For the milk mousse layer, put all the ingredients into a blender and blend until it is a smooth creamy consistency, adding more sweetener, if desired. Spread the filling over the chocolate crust and freeze for 2 hours.

To make the frosting, gently melt the coconut butter in a double boiler, then add all the remaining ingredients and stir until it is a good frosting consistency. Remove the cake from the freezer and let sit out for at least 20 minutes. Pour the frosting on top of the mousse layer, and serve.

This delicious invention is a little time consuming to prepare, but this recipe makes enough for the week and is a real hit at snack time.

BUCKWHEAT SNACK BARS

Makes 16 - Preparation time 30 minutes, plus 4 hours to sprout, 8 hours to stand, and 16 hours to dehydrate

3½ cups dry raw buckwheat or buckwheaties (already sprouted and dehydrated buckwheat)

1 cup raw almonds, soaked for 10 minutes, then drained

1 cup raw cacao powder

½ cup raw honey

2 tablespoons lucuma powder

½ cup goji berries or raisins

If using raw buckwheat, soak it in a bowl of cold water for about 4 hours, then drain in a colander and rinse thoroughly. Let stand overnight or for at least 8 hours; you will see the tails of the buckwheat emerge, then rinse again. Pour onto a Paraflexx sheet, put the sheet onto a dehydrator tray, and dehydrate at 140°F for 6 hours, or until it's crunchy.

Pour the sprouted buckwheat (or buckwheaties), soaked almonds, cacao powder, honey, and lucuma powder into a food processor and process until everything is combined and sticks together. Put the "dough" onto a Paraflexx sheet and use your hands to press it down to flatten and shape into a rectangle about ¾-inch thick. Sprinkle the goji berries or raisins on top and press them down with the back of a spoon.

Put the sheet onto a dehydrator tray and dehydrate at 120°F for 6 hours. Flip the dough over and dehydrate for an extra 4 hours, or until crunchy and firm. Cut into bars and enjoy the best raw snack that everyone will want to try.

Lucuma powder Lucuma is a delicately flavored tropical fruit, native to the cool highlands of Peru. The tree is a long-lived evergreen, which smells divine and tastes like maple syrup-flavored ice cream. Lucuma fruit is an excellent source of vitamins and minerals, rich in potassium, calcium, magnesium, and the B vitamins. It is also a very good source of beta-carotene, niacin (B3), and iron.

Lucuma powder is an amazing addition to raw chocolate and ideal for making gourmet ice cream, because it helps to combine and emulsify fats and oils with sugars and polysaccharides. Lucuma is a sweetener that does not increase your blood sugar levels, tastes delicious, and fortifies the nutritional content of your sweet inventions.

You might not think that beet and chocolate belong together, but they really are very compatible. This is a little meal in itself, packed full of iron and magnesium.

BEET AND MINT CHOC CHIP DIP

Serves 4 - Preparation time 15 minutes

2 cups fresh beets
½ cup fresh mint
2 teaspoons olive oil
½ cup raw cashew nuts
1 teaspoon raw honey
1 teaspoon apple cider vinegar
1 tablespoon tamari
1 tablespoon balsamic vinegar
¼ cup raw cacao nibs

Put the beets, mint, and olive oil into a food processor and process until it is a rice-like consistency. Spoon the mixture into a strainer and strain into a bowl to remove any excess beet juice. Place the strained mixture back into the food processor and add the remaining ingredients, except for the cacao nibs, and continue processing until you have a slightly crunchy dip consistency. Spoon into a serving bowl, sprinkle with the cacoa nibs, and enjoy with crudités.

This is a wonderful and more nutritious variation of your typical pesto recipe. Pumpkin seeds are rich in skin-feeding and immune-boosting zinc and work well with basil to combat fungal infections.

PUMPKIN PESTO

Serves 2 - Preparation time 15 minutes, plus 2 hours to soak

1 cup pumpkin seeds, soaked for 2 hours then drained
½ cup olive oil
2 garlic cloves
1 teaspoon apple cider vinegar
1 teaspoon raw honey
1 cup fresh basil leaves
1 teaspoon sea salt

Put all the ingredients into a food processor and process until very smooth.

This is delicious served with sliced tomatoes in romaine lettuce leaves with a drizzle of olive oil and balsamic vinegar. This pesto is also great added to gluten-free pasta.

These really do get super-crispy, and everyone—including the kids—will love them, especially if served with the raw zucchini hummus.

SALTY CORN CHIPS

Makes 24 - Preparation time 20 minutes, plus 20 minutes to soak, and 8–10 hours to dehydrate

1 cup whole flaxseeds, soaked for 20 minutes in ½ cup spring or filtered water, but not drained

6 cups raw corn kernels

2 tablespoons olive oil

1 garlic clove, crushed

1 teaspoon sea salt

Put the flaxseeds and water into a food processor. Add all the remaining ingredients to the food processor and process until you achieve a smooth butter consistency. Spread the mixture over 2 Paraflexx sheets, put onto the dehydrator trays, and dehydrate at 120°F for 6 hours. Flip over, and continue to dehydrate until dry, about 2–4 more hours. When dry, break into chip-sized pieces, and serve.

Our amazing friend Adi invented this tasty dip. There is a load of tahini from her Israeli roots, but greens make this hummus super healthy.

ADI'S AMAZING RAW ZUCCHINI HUMMUS

Serves 4 - Preparation time 5 minutes

1 medium zucchini or 2 small zucchini, chopped

1 cup tahini

¼ avocado, peeled and pitted

½ cup lemon juice

¼ cup olive oil

3 garlic cloves

1 rounded teaspoon sea salt

1 teaspoon ground cumin

Put all the ingredients into a blender and blend on a high speed setting until smooth. Transfer to a bowl and serve.

This is one of my favorite snacks when I am on the road—it is so light but really, really filling.

AVOCADO AND STRAWBERRY SALAD

Serves 2 - Preparation time 5 minutes

2 avocados, peeled, pitted, and sliced
2 cups of strawberries, hulled and sliced
1 tablespoon hulled hemp seeds (optional)
2 tablespoons tamari
2 tablespoons olive oil

Put the avocados and strawberries into a bowl and mix together. Add the hemp seeds, if using, tamari, and olive oil and toss together until combined. Serve.

moving on...

After two weeks of planning, we are leaving the commune today! We pack up our car and drive five hours north.

We have decided that we miss being by the water far more than we will miss the skunks and ants that had started to take over our house. But, seriously (well that was kind of serious), we have reluctantly decided that our precious family unit would be better served by being out of the commune. There are a host of reasons for this, but the key consideration has been Zella who, despite a wholehearted effort, has really not settled into commune life to her benefit.

The life we have experienced in the commune and the friends that we have met there, we will carry with us forever. At times, I have felt that I was in some kind of utopia, and other times it was more than a little challenging (due to Zella's sometimes unmanageable behavior). It has, however, been one of the most experience-rich phases of my life and made me get to know my family, especially little Z, who I do think I will parent differently from now on.

For both Jamie and myself, we feel that we do have unfinished business there, and that, at a time in our life where we will have more freedom to do so, we will undoubtedly revisit and take advantage of all the wonderful blessings that the commune has to offer. So, good-bye to a community and farewell to all you amazing creatures that live there. I feel blessed from sharing my time among you.

Another factor in our departure was the prospect of enjoying a set of new experiences. So after a fabulous five-hour journey, in which we chewed on some spectacular scenery, we have arrived in the dusty surf town of Santa Teresa in the middle of its peak season. After ten days, we decided to stay, and on that day Zella and I made some raw pizza to celebrate our new life on the beach!

Crust

½ cup raw buckwheat, soaked for 8 hours then drained and rinsed thoroughly

1 cup sunflower seeds, soaked for 8 hours then drained

1 carrot

1 celery stalk

2 garlic cloves

2 tablespoons minced red onion

¾ teaspoon sea salt

freshly ground black pepper

⅓ cup whole flaxseeds

¼ cup sesame seeds

¾ cup ground flaxseeds

1⅓ cups spring or filtered water

Tomato marinara sauce

2 dried dates, soaked for 10 minutes, then drained or 2 teaspoons raw honey

1 tomato, chopped

4 sun-dried tomatoes

½ red bell pepper, seeded and chopped (optional)

1 tablespoon olive oil

1 teaspoon apple cider vinegar

10 basil leaves (optional)

Macadamia "cheese"

1 cup raw macadamia nuts

½ cup hot spring or filtered water

2 tablespoons olive oil

1 teaspoon raw honey

1–2 tablespoons nutritional or brewer's yeast (optional)

½ teaspoon onion powder

¼ teaspoon garlic powder

½ teaspoon sea salt

1 tablespoon lemon juice

Believe it or not, pizza can be good for you! This recipe contains buckwheat, which is an amazing source of manganese, which helps to keep your bones healthy and maintain healthy blood sugar levels. Macadamias and sunflower seeds are rich in vitamin E and magnesium, and sun-dried tomatoes are a great source of iron.

RAW HEALTHY PIZZA

Serves 6 - Preparation time 30 minutes, plus 8 hours to soak, and 8 hours to dehydrate

To make the pizza crust, put the soaked, drained and rinsed buckwheat into a food processor and process until nearly smooth. Add the soaked and drained sunflower seeds and process until crumbled. Transfer the mixture to a large bowl. Put the carrot, celery, garlic, onion, salt, and black pepper into the food processor and process until well minced, then transfer to the bowl. Stir in the whole flax and sesame seeds until well combined, then add the ground flaxseeds and water and quickly stir to combine.

Make 2 crusts by halving the batter and spreading it onto 2 dehydrator trays lined with Paraflexx sheets, and dehydrate at 120°F for 4 hours, then flip and dehydrate for another 4 hours.

For the marinara sauce, put all the ingredients into a food processor or blender and process until smooth. (If you prefer, you can just garnish the pizza with chopped tomato and basil, as shown.)

For the "cheese," put all the ingredients into a blender and blend for 1–2 minutes, until it is a creamy consistency.

To assemble the pizza, spread the "cheese" over the crusts, then spread with the marinara sauce, or garnish.

dinner

DINNER

At the end of a day, as our bodies wind down and prepare for a night of sleeping, it's best to choose light meal options.

Unless you have eaten very little in the day, you'll usually have something that's small and easy to digest. Soups, lightly steamed vegetables, raw vegetable rice, or quinoa are all great options, along with raw crackers and a dip.

Occasionally, you may crave more than just a light, simple option, and so this dinner section offers some gourmet, rather more lavish, raw food menus, too. So whether you're preparing a dinner party for friends, a special dinner for the family, or just a midweek meal, you will have all bases covered.

best dinner options

Raw vegetable soups Indulge in rich, nourishing, and soothing soups. They are best served with raw crackers.

Big fruit plates This is a light, easily digestible option and allows your body to have a rest before bed.

Raw pastas with sauces and pestos Eat spiralized or very finely sliced veggies with raw sauces, because these are filling but light for this time of the day.

Crackers and dips These are a quick and easy option to fill you up in the evening.

Vegetable dishes Eat chopped and warmed nourishing seasonal vegetables with a light sauce for dinner, because these are easily digested and filling.

happiness

I believe I may actually be learning the lessons of being in the moment, of not subjugating myself to my ego, of making judgments as little as possible, and of simply appreciating everything around me, no matter how small or trivial. All of these things, and the environment that is wrapped snugly around me like a warm blanket, are contributing to some magical times. Today, I tried to pinpoint what particular thing was making me feel so happy, and in the end realized it was the sum of these parts:

- Waking up to Zella telling me "it is a beautiful day."
- Knowing that we have found the house we're going to live in for the next six months. It truly is a perfect jungle hideaway.
- Listening to Jorge Benn's indescribably feel-good album Dusty Groove while taking Zella to school.
- Making the most ecstatic afternoon chocolate smoothie, from which I believe I may still be high.
- Organizing an herb walk with my new ethno-botanist friend, who is making an inventory of all the indigenous medicine growing in this fabulous place.
- The continued blessings of my amazing new friend Adi, who has just ordered me twenty coconuts and enough organic nuts to last for the year!
- Reading Amazing Grace by David Wolfe and Nick Good, a supercool book about how to be a superhero!
- Eating the most beautiful wild green salad with mango, avocado, edible flowers, and cacao nibs.

What is the point of being ecstatic if you cannot pass the energy on? This is today's smoothie joy; I hope you get the same rush of sustained happiness as I do.

ECSTATIC SMOOTHIE

Serves 2 - Preparation time 5 minutes

- 2 cups frozen berries
- 2 bananas, peeled and coarsely chopped
- 2 tablespoons hulled hemp seeds
- 1 teaspoon mucuna powder
- 1 tablespoon raw cacao powder
- 1 tablespoon raw cacao nibs
- 1 tablespoon raw honey
- 1 tablespoon chia seeds
- 4 large edible flowers (optional)
- 1 teaspoon purple corn
- 2 cups spring or filtered water

Put all the ingredients into a blender and blend for 2 minutes, until you have a smooth thick purple chocolate hue. Pour into glasses and serve. This will keep you going for many hours!

Chia seeds I love chia seeds because they are one of the easiest, cheapest, and most nutritious foods to include in your diet. They owe their popularity to their high content of omega-3 fatty acids. They are also rich in protein, fat, and dietary fiber, and are a good source of calcium, potassium, phosphorus, sodium, and manganese. I use chia seeds to thicken smoothies or raw desserts, or I stir them into raw milk with a sprinkle of cacao for a delicious snack.

This soup is bursting with the super-antioxidant lycopene. It is also very rich and tastes extremely fresh!

QUICK RAW TOMATO SOUP

Serves 2 - Preparation time 10 minutes, plus 20 minutes to soak

4 sun-dried tomatoes, soaked for 20 minutes then drained

3 cups chopped tomatoes

1 cup chopped, seeded red bell pepper

½ garlic clove

1 teaspoon hulled hemp seeds or 10 raw cashew nuts

½ teaspoon sea salt

½ cup fresh basil leaves

1 tablespoon avocado flesh, chopped

Put all the ingredients, except the basil and avocado, into a blender and blend until smooth and creamy. Add the basil to the blender and pulse a few times until just chopped. Serve immediately in bowls, with the chopped avocado on top.

This is a mellow and kid-friendly guacamole!

GUACAMOLE

Serves 2-4 - Preparation time 5 minutes

Guacamole

2 avocados, peeled, and pitted

1 tomato, chopped

½ white onion, chopped

1 garlic clove

1 lime, juiced

1 tablespoon olive oil

¼ teaspoon sea salt

Topping

1 cup chopped tomatoes

½ cup fresh cilantro

Put all the ingredients for the guacamole into a blender and blend until smooth and creamy. Transfer to a bowl or use as a filling for the Raw Corn Tacos (see right), topped off with the tomatoes and fresh cilantro, and serve immediately.

Everyone loves these! They're a wholesome, satisfying replacement for enchiladas and tortillas. Fill with Guacamole, chopped tomatoes, and cilantro—heaven!

RAW CORN TACOS

Serves 6 - Preparation time 25 minutes, plus 8 hours to dehydrate

3 cups fresh corn kernels

½ cup ground flaxseeds

½ cup spring or filtered water

¼ cup chopped onion

1 tablespoon raw honey

1 garlic clove, crushed

1 teaspoon ground cumin

½ teaspoon sea salt

Put all the ingredients into a food processor and process until you achieve a smooth yellowy consistency.

Pour small tortilla-size portions onto Paraflexx sheets, about 6 per sheet, making sure they are not too thin, otherwise they will split when you flip them.

Put the sheets onto dehydrator trays and dehydrate at 115°F for 4 hours. Flip them over and dehydrate for an additional 4 hours.

You can store these for 3 days in an airtight container.

I often try to re-create favorite pasta dishes using only vegetables. You certainly won't miss wheat pasta after you've tasted this flavorful version.

SPIRALIZED ZUCCHINI WITH NUTRIENT-RICH PASTA SAUCE

Serves 2 - Preparation time 20 minutes, plus 10 minutes to soak and 30 minutes to marinate

For the pasta, spiralize the zucchini following the directions provided with the spiralizer you're using. Once spiralized, place the zucchini in a shallow dish, add the lemon juice and olive oil, toss to coat, and let marinate for 30 minutes.

For the sauce, put all the ingredients into a blender and blend until you have a smooth creamy tomato sauce.

Pour the sauce over the marinated zucchini and serve.

Tip If you don't have a very powerful blender, press the oil, vinegar, and chopped tomato down into the bottom of the blender so it's easier to blend, then add the bell pepper and avocado and the remaining sauce ingredients.

Pasta

4 zucchini

2 tablespoons lemon juice

2 tablespoons olive oil

Sauce

2 tablespoons goji berries, soaked for 10 minutes, then drained, or 2 dried dates, soaked for 10 minutes, then drained

1 tomato, chopped

½ red bell pepper, seeded

1 cup fresh basil leaves

8 sun-dried tomatoes (optional)

1 tablespoon avocado flesh

2 tablespoons olive oil

1 teaspoon apple cider vinegar

1 garlic clove

a pinch of sea salt

This rice is as close as you'll come to real fried rice. It's got the right balance of mouthfeel and taste, and it is a winner with all the family. The stir-fry is a delicious dish, which is full of loads of cancer-fighting cruciferous vegetables with a delicate sweet and savory sauce.

Stir-fry

2 tablespoons broccoli florets

1 cup shredded savoy or green cabbage

1 whole cauliflower, broken into florets

½ cup mung bean sprouts

2 red bell peppers, seeded, and cut into julienne

2 carrots, peeled, and cut into julienne

3 tablespoons olive oil

2 teaspoons agave nectar

2 teaspoons tamari

1 tablespoon cider vinegar

a pinch of dried red pepper flakes (optional)

1 tablespoon black sesame seeds

Rice

1 whole cauliflower, broken into florets

½ cup raw cashew nuts

2 tablespoons chopped white onion

2 garlic cloves

¼ cup fresh cilantro leaves

3 tablespoons olive oil

1 tablespoon Bragg's Amino Acids or tamari

RAW CAULIFLOWER RICE
WITH STIR-FRY VEGETABLES

Serves 4 - Preparation time 25 minutes, plus 6 hours to dehydrate

Optional but awesome! Warm all the ingredients for the cauliflower rice in a saucepan on very low heat, stirring constantly, until just warm to the touch. Alternatively, place all the rice ingredients on a Paraflexx sheet, put onto a dehydrator tray, and dehydrate at 120°F for 30 minutes.

To make the stir-fry, put all the vegetables into a large bowl and mix together. Add the olive oil, agave nectar, tamari, vinegar, red pepper flakes, and black sesame seeds and toss until coated. Put the mixture onto several Paraflexx sheets, then put them onto dehydrator trays and dehydrate at 140°F for 1 hour or more, depending on how soft you like your vegetables. It takes 6 hours for them to have a cooked feel.

For the rice, put the second, broken cauliflower and the cashew nuts into a food processor and pulse into "rice," then transfer to a bowl. Put the onion, garlic, and cilantro into the food processor and pulse until finely chopped. Stir the mixture into the cauliflower and mix well. Drizzle the olive oil and Bragg's Amino Acids or tamari over the top and enjoy with the stir-fried vegetables!

a celebration

The idea has been simmering in my mind for a couple of weeks now, but it never raised its head above the parapet. Now I am conscious of it: a party, a celebration.

It has been some time coming, but finally I feel settled. I feel very much alive, very "in tune." Things are just falling into place: Zella and school; Djuna and her love of the beach; nature; comfort; friends; and food. Friends and food . . . certainly something that goes together!

I have spent the last two weeks planning an amazing party full of high-vibrational food and drink with my gorgeous friend Adi. She has a very special quality, among many, and that is to thank the universe for everything at all times, whether it be good or bad. She is Israeli and follows the traditional Jewish celebrations, so is more than qualified to know how to make an occasion special.

We have honored the jungle in choosing mostly foods that are indigenous to this country, and we created a three-course raw food dinner.

Today is the day for eating and drinking the highly vibrational, but delicious and decadent food. It is also a day of thanks, thanks to the jungle, thanks to our house, and thanks to Costa Rica for our amazing time here.

THE MENU

Raw Cannelloni with
  Red Cashew Cheese

Pineapple and
  Cucumber Gazpacho

Raw Lasagna with Wild Green
  Salad and Edible Flowers

Coconut Cream Pie

These delicious canapés are light but very satisfying and full of flavor.

RAW CANNELLONI
WITH RED CASHEW CHEESE

Serves 6 - Preparation time 1 hour, plus 3½ hours to dehydrate

6 zucchini, thinly sliced lengthwise
⅓ cup olive oil, plus extra for brushing
2 cups chopped leeks
2 cups chopped portobello mushrooms
(or any preferred mushrooms)
2 tablespoons lemon juice
1 teaspoon raw honey
¼ teaspoon sea salt
1 cup Red Cashew Cheese Dip (see page 104)
edible flowers, to serve

Brush the thinly sliced zucchini strips with olive oil and place on a Paraflexx sheet. Put the sheet onto a dehydrator tray and dehydrate at 120°F for 1 hour. Meanwhile, toss the leeks and mushrooms in the olive oil, lemon juice, honey, and salt and mix well, then place on a Paraflexx sheet. Put the sheet onto a dehydrator tray and dehydrate at 140°F for 2 hours.

When ready to prepare your canapés, spread 1 teaspoon of Red Cashew Cheese Dip on each zucchini strip and spoon a little of the leek and mushroom mixture on top. Roll into cannelloni-style rolls and place on a Paraflexx sheet. Put the sheet onto a dehydrator tray and dehydrate at 120°F for 30 minutes before serving. Sprinkle with edible flowers.

Vitamin A-rich red bell peppers give this savory dish a delicious sweet but slightly earthy kick.

RED CASHEW
CHEESE DIP

Serves 2–3 - Preparation time 10 minutes, plus 20 minutes to soak

1 cup raw cashew nuts, soaked for 20 minutes then drained
½ cup Morning Nut Milk (see page 35) or other nut milk, or water (the milk makes it a little bit creamier)
½ red bell pepper, seeded
1 tablespoon lemon juice
1 teaspoon raw honey
½ garlic clove
1 tablespoon nutritional yeast (optional)

Put all the ingredients into a blender and blend until you achieve a smooth creamy consistency.

This will keep in the refrigerator for 3 days.

These little canapé shots are so refreshing and sweet, but have a great chile kick.

PINEAPPLE AND CUCUMBER
GAZPACHO

Serves 6 - Preparation time 20 minutes

2 pineapples, peeled and chopped
4 cucumbers, juiced in a juicer
½ jalapeño chile, chopped
1 bunch of fresh cilantro, chopped
1 bunch of fresh mint, chopped

Put the pineapple, cucumber juice, and chile into a blender and process until you achieve a chunky consistency. Then throw in the herbs and blend again until it is a creamy smoothie-like consistency. Add more chile, if you prefer, then serve in chilled shot glasses.

I always try and make my salads as fresh and wild as possible. Try throwing in a few wild greens or edible flowers from the garden—a huge nutritional upgrade!

WILD GREEN SALAD

AND CITRUS TAHINI DRESSING

Serves 6 - Preparation time 15 minutes

Salad

2 bunches of wild arugula

2 bunches of spinach

¼ cup chopped fresh mint (or whatever fresh herbs you have growing)

4 avocados, peeled, pitted, and chopped

6 hibiscus flowers, chopped, or whatever edible flowers you have growing (optional)

Dressing

½ cup olive oil

⅓ cup lemon juice

⅓ cup freshly squeezed orange juice

½ teaspoon sea salt

3 tablespoons tahini

Mix all the salad ingredients together in a bowl.

For the dressing, put all the ingredients into a small blender or food processor and process until smooth. Serve with the salad.

I love to make raw lasagna because it always looks so beautiful and is absolutely bursting with the taste of summer. It is a great first dish to give to non-raw foodies.

RAW LASAGNA

Serves 6 - Preparation time 1 hour, plus 4 hours to soak, and 2 hours to marinate

Tomato sauce

2 cups sun-dried tomatoes, soaked for 4 hours then drained

2 dried dates, soaked for 10 minutes, then drained, or 1 tablespoon raw honey or natural sweetener

2 tomatoes, chopped

½ white onion, chopped

½ cup olive oil

1 teaspoon sea salt

½ teaspoon paprika

Pasta

6 zucchini, thinly sliced lengthwise

6 tomatoes, thinly sliced

½ cup olive oil, plus extra for drizzling

1 teaspoon sea salt

balsamic vinegar, for drizzling

1 tablespoon dried oregano

"Cheese"

2 cups raw cashew nuts or pine nuts

2 tablespoons lemon juice

2 tablespoons nutritional yeast

1 teaspoon salt

¾ cup spring or filtered water, or more if needed

½ garlic clove

Pesto

2 cups fresh basil leaves

½ cup olive oil

1 garlic clove

1 teaspoon salt

1 teaspoon raw honey

1 tablespoon apple cider vinegar

1 tablespoon lemon juice

½ cup pine nuts or hulled hemp seeds

For the pasta, put the zucchini and tomatoes into a shallow dish, add the olive oil and salt, toss until coated, and let marinate for up to 2 hours.

For the tomato sauce and the "cheese" put all the ingredients for each separately into a blender and blend until smooth. Set aside.

Put all the ingredients for the pesto, except the pine nuts or hemp seeds, into a food processor and process briefly. Add the pine nuts or hemp seeds through the feeder tube and process until a pesto-like consistency is achieved.

Remove the zucchini and tomatoes from the marinade and put the zucchini strips on the bottom of a lasagna dish, followed by a layer of tomato sauce, then "cheese," then 4 dollops of pesto. Arrange a layer of the tomatoes on top, then repeat, finishing with a thin layer of tomatoes. Drizzle with a little olive oil and balsamic vinegar and a sprinkling of oregano.

This pie makes me think of a perfect English summer's day. It is a fresh and yet deliciously decadent coconut variation of strawberries and cream that's actually good for you.

COCONUT CREAM PIE

Serves 6 – Preparation time 1 hour, plus 10 minutes to soak, 12–16 hours to dehydrate, and 2 hours to chill

Crust

1 cup blanched almonds, soaked for 10 minutes, then drained

1½ cups raw cashew nuts

⅓ cup raw honey

¼ teaspoon salt

Filling

1¾ cups canned coconut milk

4 teaspoons coconut palm sugar

⅓ vanilla bean, split lengthwise and seeds scraped out

1–2 cups strawberry preserve (coarsely purée the strawberries or buy a sugar-free preserve; both are delicious)

2 cups mixed berries

For the crust, put all the ingredients into a food processor and process for 1–2 minutes, until the mixture starts sticking together and forms a ball. Divide the dough into six equal pieces for 5–5½-inch pie shells. Place plastic wrap in individual tart pans, dampen your hands, and spread the dough in the pans.

Place the tart pans on Paraflexx sheets, then put them onto dehydrator trays and dehydrate at 140°F for 12 hours. After 8 hours, remove the crusts from the tart pans to dehydrate them evenly, but make sure they are hard enough and won't collapse. They might need to be dehydrated for an extra 2–4 hours.

To make the filling, chill the can of coconut milk for at least 2 hours, then scoop out the coconut fat that separates out and solidifies (leaving the watery liquid behind), and whip it just like whipped cream. Put it into a food processor with the sugar and vanilla and process for at least 3–4 minutes, until it's really thick. Transfer to a bowl and chill if not serving immediately. Spread the preserves on the pie shells very carefully, then arrange the whipped filling on top and finish with fresh berries to serve.

This is a deliciously refreshing
fizzy apple drink.

APPLE AID

Serves 6 - Preparation time 15 minutes

20 apples, juiced in a juicer
4 cups sparkling water
10 limes, squeezed
3 drops of stevia (optional)

Mix all the ingredients in a large pitcher, and serve
immediately.

Not only does this drink look beautiful,
it also provides energy.

GINGERED
WATERMELON JUICE

Serves 6 - Preparation time 10 minutes

2 watermelons, peeled
1-inch piece of fresh ginger, peeled

If you like, juice everything—even the seeds and rind—and
you'll get a beautiful pink and green beverage. If you want
to make it alcoholic, a shot of raw vodka works perfectly!

Serve in a large pitcher with ice.

remedies

to be in the moment

I was playing hide-and-seek with Zella and her friends on the beach when I suddenly felt a burning sensation on the soles of my feet. In the blink of an eye, this sensation deeply intensified, and I looked down to find I was standing ankle deep in burning coals. I knew even when I started running full tilt toward the ocean that this would make things worse, but the pain was already unbearable and I needed the coolness of water. I actually needed cold water and aloe, but where was it going to come from?

After much running around and Zella shouting at everyone that we needed some "aloe-bird-cream-water," a blessing arrived in the form of two lovely Tica boys holding a bucket of water and an aloe plant! Yes, really—I couldn't believe my eyes! They had seen everything that was going on from the back of the beach. They helped me so much I could have cried. What then kept running through my mind was how on earth I was going to get home. I knew my friend couldn't drive, and I had a ten-month-old and two three-year-olds to get home. At this point, yet another huge blessing arrived: Mitra and Raneka, two of the loveliest people who lived with us in the commune. Mitra is an acupuncturist and healer and was so amazing with me, helping me breathe through the pain while he applied the weirdest looking burn cream. Raneka drove my car and took the girls home, and all was taken care of—wow!

Aloe has been a terrific help in healing what have turned out to be second-degree burns to both of my feet, and thankfully there is an abundant supply of it around me. I am applying aloe twice daily underneath some light gauze wrapping.

After one week, I have made a miraculous recovery. Incredibly, I am able to run now! Thank you, aloe!

This blend of goodies delivers high amounts of vitamin E designed to help prevent scarring, and vitamin C to boost collagen production. It is also a fantastic daily tonic to help boost the body's healing ability. Colloidal silver is a suspension of submicroscopic metallic silver particles in distilled water that acts as a natural antibiotic to help protect against any kind of infection and has been used for centuries to kill bacteria and viruses.

Magic aloe More than 300 species of aloe exist, but it is <u>Aloe</u> <u>barbadensis</u> that is considered the most nutritionally and medicinally potent variety. Aloe vera contains 20 of the 22 essential amino acids, 8 of the 13 known vitamins, and is high in antioxidants, enzymes, and minerals. It is also beneficial to the digestive system: it acts as a mild lubricant, has a mild laxative effect, and due to its cooling effect, is fantastic at treating all disorders associated with heat, such as heartburn, indigestion, and stomach inflammation. Aloe is also a cell regenerator that reduces the healing time of external and internal wounds, inhibits scarring, and has analgesic and antiseptic effects.

CREAMY
ALOE DRINK

Serves 2 - Preparation time 5 minutes

2 tablespoons fresh aloe gel
½ avocado, peeled, and pitted (rich in vitamin E)
1 cup leafy greens
1 celery stalk
½ cucumber, peeled and coarsely chopped
juice of 2 oranges
1 teaspoon camu camu (South American berry, very rich in vitamin C)
1 mango, peeled, pitted, and chopped
1 teaspoon colloidal silver
2 cups spring or filtered water

Put all the ingredients into a blender and blend for 1–2 minutes. Pour into glasses and serve.

Thanks to an unreasonable corrugated plastic roof and a dead skunk, I ended up with an old stunt girl injury—two broken ribs. Subsequently, I acquired an unpleasant lung infection and was ordered to take antibiotics. This was the powerful natural antibiotic drink I came up with. Suffice to say, it took me three weeks to recover, but no pharmaceuticals were needed!

MY JUNGLE ANTIBIOTIC DRINK

Serves 2 - Preparation time 10 minutes, plus 10 minutes to cool

2 lemongrass stalks

2 cups spring or filtered water

½-inch piece of fresh ginger, peeled and chopped (antimicrobial)

½-inch piece of turmeric, peeled and chopped (antimicrobial, antibiotic actions)

½ crushed garlic clove (antibiotic, antibacterial)

2 limes, juiced (rich in vitamin C)

10 drops of propolis (antibiotic)

2 tablespoons raw honey (antibacterial)

½ cup maracuya juice or standard passion fruit juice (helps reduce mucus)

Boil the lemongrass in the water for 10 minutes, then strain. Add the ginger, turmeric, and garlic to the strained lemongrass tea, then squeeze in the lime juice. Add the propolis, honey, and maracuya or passion fruit juice. Pour the mixture into a blender and blend for 1 minute. Pour through a strainer and let cool for 10 minutes. Once cool, pour into a glass bottle or jar. This can be stored for 3 days.

Pau d'Arco helps to flush out fermentation in the digestive tract (one of the causes of severe jet lag) so its inclusion in this recipe for "magic tea," which can be drunk any time of the day, is perfect. If you are on blood-thinning medication, check with your doctor before taking Pau d'Arco.

A.M./P.M. MAGIC TEA

Serves 2–4 - Preparation time 5 minutes

4 cups spring or filtered water
4 teaspoons Pau d'Arco tea leaves
stevia or raw honey, to taste (optional)

Boil the water, then put the tea leaves in a cup and pour the boiling water over them. I like to make this before bed, so we have our tea at room temperature the next morning. The tea makes a great liquid base for smoothies, and the kids also love it because it's slightly sweet and earthy. Drink either hot or cold, sweetened to taste.

This is our fabulous herbal tea savior, which calms the nervous system and helps regulate sleep. It is a real must for teething or for little ones who aren't very well.

SLEEP EASY

Serves 2–4 - Preparation time 5 minutes

6 cups spring or filtered water
2 teaspoons passion flower tea
2 teaspoons chamomile tea
2 drops of valerian tincture
raw honey, or stevia, to taste (optional)

Heat the water, then pour it over the tea and let steep for 3 minutes. Strain, then add the valerian drops. This is enough to treat the whole family but works wonders with little ones—omit the valerian if using for more than 2 consecutive nights. To sweeten, add a little honey or a few drops of stevia.

ONION AND THYME COUGH SYRUP

This is a great cough remedy. Onions work in a similar way to garlic and they have strong antimicrobial properties. Thyme is a great antiseptic and works as an expectorant to loosen and expel mucus.

Makes 20–30 servings - Preparation time 20 minutes, plus 8 hours to steep

2–3 fresh thyme sprigs
1 white onion, finely diced
2–3 tablespoons raw honey
scant ½ cup hot water

Using a mortar and pestle, pound the thyme to a fine consistency. Transfer to a bowl, add the onion, and mix together. Add the honey and hot water and let steep for eight hours, then strain.

Store in a sealed jar in a cool dark place for up to 1 month.

Dosage

- Adults 1 teaspoon, five times a day
- Children 1 teaspoon, twice a day

I found some kids' probiotics envelopes in my luggage, so I thought this would be a perfect time to make probiotic coconut water; it's a fabulous fermented drink to help maintain happy stomachs! This is one of the cheapest, easiest ways to maintain your healthy bacteria.

COCOBIOTIC
DRINK

Makes 20 servings - Preparation time 5 minutes, plus 12 hours to ferment

1 envelope of probiotics
1 cup coconut water
1 clean open-mouthed glass jar
1 dish towel

Put the probiotics and coconut water into a blender and blend briefly until mixed. Pour the mixture into a glass jar, leave the lid off, and wrap in a dish towel. Let stand for 12 hours, then cover and refrigerate.

This keeps for 5 days. Adults can drink this liberally, but kids need only 1–2 tablespoons each day.

This was my daily smoothie once I had recovered from that nasty lung infection. It is a great chocolate drink packed full of adaptogenic herbs (see sidebar, right) to rebuild an exhausted body.

LET
CHOCOLATE
BE THY BERRY
MEDICINE

Serves 1–2 - Preparation time 5 minutes

1 teaspoon ashwagandha powder

1 teaspoon shatavari powder

2 scoops of Sunwarrior or hemp protein powder (or any preferred protein powder)

2 cups Morning Nut Milk (see page 35) or other nut milk, or spring or filtered water

1 tablespoon raw honey

1 tablespoon raw cacao nibs

1 cup fresh blueberries or pitted cherries

1 tablespoon coconut butter

Put all the powders into a blender first, then add the liquid, honey, and remaining ingredients and blend for a minute or so. This is a tonic medicine that will keep you going for hours.

I have one of these a day, and change the herbs accordingly. These tonics are particularly nourishing for the nervous and reproductive systems and really help jump-start the day!

Ashwagandha and Shatavari Ashwagandha root is renowned for "imparting the strength of a stallion." In Ayurveda, it is considered to be an adaptogenic herb, meaning that it helps the body attain the correct balance. It is known more as a male tonic herb, but is also a fantastic restorative for women. It's used as a tonic that both strengthens and calms. Its Latin name Somnifera implies its calming properties, while helping the body and mind to adapt to the stresses of modern living. It grows all over India as a biennial root that burrows deep into the ground, and although it is known as "Indian ginseng" because of its similar resemblance and strengthening properties, it is not stimulating.

Shatavari translates, as "she who possesses 100 husbands" and is perhaps best known as a female "rejuvenative." It is useful for treating infertility, decreased libido, premenstrual syndrome (PMS), and menopause, but it can also treat impotence and general sexual debility. In addition to its applications for reproductive organs, shatavari is also effective for treating stomach ulcers, hyperacidity, and diarrhea. Dry and irritated membranes in the upper respiratory tract are soothed by this herb, so it is useful in bronchitis and chronic fevers. It is believed to bring into balance all of the body's fluids.

These two tonic herbs complement each other in action and are great for people going through very stressful times. These are the herbs I use the most for myself, my kids, and my patients because they are strengthening and an easy regular addition to smoothies, shakes, and hot drinks.

first aid

We love to travel light, but no matter how lightly we travel, I always carry along a natural first-aid kit. Being prepared with my favorite remedies gives me peace of mind on the road and keeps me from having to search out natural products in acute situations. These are my essentials, aside from the usual bandages and dressings, etc., which should be included in any first-aid kit. Be sure to buy pure essential oils, not fragrance oils.

- Antibiotic tincture: Echinacea and Andrographis.
- Arnica cream/gel: Fantastic for sprains and strains.
- Bentonite clay: This is great to mix with water to make a topical application for skin infections.
- Calendula-comfrey salve: An astringent, antibacterial, antifungal, and anti-inflammatory, and a great wound-healing remedy.
- Chamomile tea bags: This tea is great for calming, and is especially good for little ones.
- Charcoal pills: Essential in cases of food poisoning or if anyone has eaten anything toxic. Also useful for diarrhea in adults.
- Colloidal silver pills or solution: A wonderfully safe natural antibiotic for every type of illness.
- Grapefruit seed extract (GSE): Essential for upset stomachs, food poisoning. Use 1 drop a day for children and 3 drops a day for adults as a preventative while traveling.
- Hypericum and calendula tincture: The best wound cleaner ever.
- Iodine: Use topically for cuts and grazes and internally for infection.
- Neem oil and cream: Fantastic for bites, a great antifungal and antibacterial cream.
- Pau d'Arco powder or tea bags: Antiviral, antibacterial, and antifungal, a great tonic for the immune system.
- Siberian ginseng capsules: Energy giving, and they support adrenal energy; they also help to combat radiation.
- Tea tree oil: Dilute and use to clean wounds. It is also useful to sterilize surfaces and tweezers.
- Witch hazel extract: Both antiseptic and anti-inflammatory, so useful for insect bites and skin irritations. It is also fantastic for bumps and bruises.

This is the number one recipe we use at home when there are the first signs of tickly sore throat, because it fights off the early stages of a cold or flu and works wonders!

MY INDIAN GODDESS SYRUP

2 garlic cloves
1 teaspoon fresh or ground turmeric
½ lemon
1–2 tablespoons raw honey

First, crush the garlic cloves into a bowl. This releases the allicin in the garlic, which is a natural antibiotic. Add the turmeric and mix until it forms a paste. The curcumin in the turmeric is an antioxidant, which is great for the immune system. Squeeze in the lemon half, the antiseptic qualities of which are great for sore throats, and mix well. Add some honey; you can use as much or as little as you like. Stir well, then pass the mixture through a strainer to get rid of any chunks of garlic.

Dosage

- Adults 3 teaspoons, twice a day
- Children 2 teaspoons, twice a day
- For children under 2 years, take ½ teaspoon ground cinnamon in a little water every 2 hours, plus 5 drops of Echinacea three times a day.

headache remedies

- Drink chamomile tea as often as desired (it's a great anti-inflammatory).
- Drink coconut water to rehydrate.
- Massage 2 drops of diluted peppermint essential oil onto your temples, forehead, and neck (Keep away from eyes.)

The volatile oils in ginger have long been used as a carminative on the digestive system, soothing nausea and stomach discomfort.

GINGER TEA

2 cups hot spring or filtered water
½-inch piece of fresh ginger, peeled and grated
1 tablespoon raw honey

Pour the hot water over the ginger and let steep for 5 minutes before adding the honey. Drink freely.

To avoid motion or travel sickness, take 6 capsules of powdered ginger about 45 minutes before departing.

SUPPLIERS

United States

Longevity Warehouse
Tel: 1-805-870-5756
www.longevitywarehouse.com

Sunwarrior
Tel: 888-540-3667
www.sunwarrior.com

IHerb.com
17825 Indian Street
Moreno Valley, CA 92551
Tel: 951-616-3600
www.iherb.com

Canada

Real Raw Food
15-A-2
Naramata, BC, Canada
V0H 1N0
Tel: 250-496-5215
www.realrawfood.com

United Kingdom

Detox Your World
9/10 Morton Peto Estate
(off Morton Peto Road)
Great Yarmouth
Norfolk NR31 0LT
Tel: 08700 113 119
www.detoxyourworld.com

Raw Living
Tel: 01243 523335
www.rawliving.eu

Aggressive Health
Tel: 01933 221736
www.aggressivehealth.co.uk

The publisher would like to thank
UK Juicers for the loan of equipment
used during the photoshoot.

RECOMMENDED READING

Boutenko V., *Green For Life* (North Atlantic Books, Berkeley, CA, 2010)

Grauds C., *Jungle Medicine* (The Center For Spirited Medicine, San Rafael, CA, 2004)

McIntyre A., *Herbal Treatment of Children: Western and Ayurvedic Perspectives* (Butterworth-Heinemann Ltd., Gloucestershire, UK, 2005)

Melngailis S., *Living Raw Food* (HarperCollins, New York, NY, 2009)

Ober C., Sinatra S. T., Zucker M., *Earthing: The Most Important Health Discovery Ever?* (Basic Health Publications, Laguna Beach, CA, 2010)

Shazzie, *Evie's Kitchen: Raising an Ecstatic Child* (RawCreation, Norfolk, UK, 2008)

Sircus M., *Iodine: Bringing Back the Universal Medicine* (IMVA, Joao Pessoa, Brazil, 2010)

Tierra M., *Planetary Herbology* (Lotus Press, New York, NY, 1992)

Winston D., *Adaptogens: Herbs for Strength, Stamina, and Stress Relief* (Healing Arts Press, Rochester, VT, 2007)

Wolfe D, and Good N., *Amazing Grace: The Nine Principles of Living in Natural Magic* (North Atlantic Books, Berkeley, CA, 2008)

Wolfe D. and Maimes S., *Superfoods: The Food and Medicine of the Future* (North Atlantic Books, Berkeley, CA, 2009)

Wood K. *Raw Magic: Recipes for the Revolution* (RawCreation, Norfolk, UK, 2008)

Wren B., *Cellular Awakening: How Your Body Holds and Creates Light* (Hay House, London, 2009)

USEFUL WEBSITES

My website
www.anneliewhitfield.com

Living Libations
www.livinglibations.com

SuperHero Training Creators
www.successultranow.com

IMVA International Medical Veritas Association
www.imva.info

PachaMama
www.pachamama.com

INDEX

A

Adi's Amazing Raw Zucchini Hummus 82
Almond Crunch Cookies 71
aloe 115
A.M./P.M. Magic Tea 118
Apple Ade 111
Apple and Date Granola 20
ashwagandha 122
Avocado and Strawberry Salad 84

B

Beet and Mint Choc Chip Dip 81
Berry Crazy 26
Best-Ever Buckwheat Cereal 30
Buckwheat Snack Bars 78

C

Cacao Shot Mix 65
Cheesecake for Breakfast 23
chia seeds 93
Chocolate Tropical Kebab Sticks 72
Cocobiotic Drink 121
Coconut Cream Pie 108
coconut oil 36
Creamy Aloe Drink 115
Creamy Banana Chocolate Breakfast 33
Crunchy Chocolate Hearts 68
Cucumber and Mint Summer Soup 57

D

Dairy-Free Fruit Yogurt 52
Detox Pineapple Shake 29

E

Ecstatic Smoothie 93
equipment 11

F

first aid 124
Flax Hemp Bars 71
Full Spectrum Chocolate Birthday Cake 76

G

Ginger Tea 125
Gingered Watermelon Juice 111
goji berries 52
Guacamole 96

H

headache remedies 125
hemp seeds 29
Hempy Burritos 44

K

Kids Go Crackers 51

L

Let Chocolate Be Thy Berry Medicine 122
lucuma powder 78

M

maca 66
magnesium 58
Magnesium Lunch Crunch Smoothie 58
Mango, Avocado, and Tomato Burritos 44
Mango Lassi Mousse with Berries 36
medicinal mushrooms 26
Morning Nut Milk 35
Morning Sun Juice 18
mucuna powder 35
My Indian Goddess Syrup 125
My Jungle Antibiotic Drink 116

O

Onion and Thyme Cough Syrup 120

P

Pau d'Arco 118
Pineapple and Cucumber Gazpacho 104
Pour Down the Pink Protein 36
Protein-Rich Sandwich Bread 48
Pumpkin Pesto 81

Q

Quick Raw Tomato Soup 95
Quinoa Sprouts, Avocado, and Tomato Marinara Wraps 54

R

raw cacao 68
Raw Cannelloni with Red Cashew Cheese 103
Raw Cauliflower Rice with Stir-Fry Vegetables 101
Raw Chocolate Chip Nutrient-Rich Cookies 51
Raw Corn Tacos 96
Raw Healthy Pizza 86
Raw Iced Mochachino 35
Raw Lasagna 106
Raw Vanilla Ice Cream 74
Red Cashew Cheese Dip 104

S

Salty Corn Chips 82
shatavari 122
Sleep Easy 118
Spiralized Zucchini with Nutrient-Rich Pasta Sauce 98
Super Seaweed Salad 47

T

Tropical Doorstep Smoothie 17
Tropical Salad of Love 43

W

Wild Green Salad and Citrus Tahini Dressing 105

Z

Zella's Best Chocolate Orange Balls 66

acknowledgments

First, I have to thank my wonderful parents for the gifts they have bestowed upon me; the beautiful farm on which I grew up and became inspired; and allowing me to be me despite my sometimes crazy choices. Thank you to my beautiful husband Jamie, who has shown me only endless support and understanding in my pursuit to live the healthiest and most natural way possible, coping with my crazy and sometimes incessant chatter about natural living, and for always being committed to our beautiful family. Thank you to my gorgeous and awe-inspiring little girls, Zella and Djuna, who are the perfect example of pure _energy_. Thank you to my special and supportive friends and, of course, those hugely knowledgeable and brave warrior folk. I have learned so, _so_ much.

Special blessings to the nutrient-rich foods that have nourished me, the wild foods that have grounded me, and the plant spirits for guiding me.

Adi Mayer you're my angel!